The Conversation on Gender Diversity

Critical Conversations

Martin LaMonica, Series Editor

The Conversation U.S. is an independent, nonprofit news organization dedicated to delivering expert knowledge to the public through journalism. Every day The Conversation produces 10–12 stories through a collaboration between scholars and editors, with the scholars writing explanatory journalism and analysis based on their research and the editors helping them translate it into plain language. The articles can be read on TheConversation.com and have been republished by more than a thousand newspapers and websites through a Creative Commons license, meaning that the content is always free to read and republish.

The book series Critical Conversations is published collaboratively by The Conversation U.S. and Johns Hopkins University Press. Each volume in the series features a curated selection of subject–specific articles from The Conversation and is guest-edited by an expert scholar of the subject.

■

The Conversation on Gender Diversity is guest-edited by Jules Gill–Peterson, a scholar of transgender history and the author of *Histories of the Transgender Child* (University of Minnesota Press, 2018), which won a Lambda Literary Award for Transgender Nonfiction and the Children's Literature Association Book Award.

Martin LaMonica is Executive Editor and Project Manager.
Kira Barrett is Editorial Assistant.
Gita Zimmerman is Illustrator of the part-title images, overseen
    by Conversation Marketing and Communications Manager
    Anissa Cooke-Batista.
Beth Daley is Editor and General Manager of The Conversation U.S.
Bruce Wilson is Chief Innovation and Development Officer of
    The Conversation U.S.

We would like to express our gratitude to the editors and scholars who produced the articles collected here and to thank our colleagues and funders who allow us to do this important work in the public interest.

THE CONVERSATION

on Gender Diversity

edited by Jules Gill-Peterson

Johns Hopkins University Press
BALTIMORE

Johns Hopkins University Press
2715 North Charles Street
Baltimore, Maryland 21218
www.press.jhu.edu

Library of Congress Cataloging-in-Publication Data

Names: Gill-Peterson, Jules, editor.
Title: The conversation on gender diversity / edited by Jules Gill-Peterson.
Description: Baltimore, Maryland : Johns Hopkins University Press, 2023. |
   Series: Critical conversations | Includes bibliographical references and
   index.
Identifiers: LCCN 2022024607 | ISBN 9781421446189 (paperback) | ISBN
   9781421446196 (ebook)
Subjects: LCSH: Transgender people—United States. | Gender
   identity—United States. | Gender-nonconforming people—United States. |
   BISAC: SOCIAL SCIENCE / Gender Studies | POLITICAL SCIENCE / Public
   Policy / Social Policy
Classification: LCC HQ77.95.U6 C37 2023 | DDC 306.76/8—dc23/eng/
   20220831
LC record available at https://lccn.loc.gov/2022024607

A catalog record for this book is available from the British Library.

Special discounts are available for bulk purchases of this book.
For more information, please contact Special Sales at
specialsales@jh.edu.

Contents

Part V.
Trans Rights Are Human Rights,
but Rights Are Not Enough 190

First, a Quick Story

IN THE FALL OF 2014, my wife sent me a listing for an environment and energy editor job at a place called The Conversation. I had vaguely heard of this outfit, one of many startups trying to innovate within the troubled world of journalism. As a longtime reporter and editor, I had little optimism that anyone could fix the media's broken business model. But I was intrigued by the organization's approach of having college professors and researchers fill the gap left by layoff after layoff of experienced reporters. I emailed the managing editor and landed an interview.

Days after I left the interview held in a cramped basement office on the Boston University campus, the mission underpinning the venture—to improve the public discourse—stayed with me. Could academics, working with journalists, help fulfill the vital role of journalism to inform the public by sharing more facts and knowledge?

As I now write this foreword years later, I can say that the power of The Conversation's founding idea and novel editorial model endures. And millions of people benefit every day. A media nonprofit with editions in multiple countries, we publish daily news analysis and explanatory journalism that comes out of a collaboration between academics and journalists. Put another way, it's like a digital newspaper whose reporters are researchers and professors with deep subject expertise and whose editors are journalists who themselves are topic specialists with years of experience covering the news.

We have a website, multiple email newsletters, and many outposts on social media. Why make a book from our daily journalism? And who would want to read it?

As an independent media nonprofit, we exist to serve the public with accurate and reliable information you can use to navigate an increasingly complex world. We are funded by universities, foundations, and individual donors. This collection's contributions are grounded in academic research, since the authors—sometimes people who have worked in their field for decades—are writing about their areas of expertise. There are citations to peer-reviewed articles and books throughout, and this collection itself has gone through peer review.

But this rich information is also accessible. Working with journalist-editors, the academics write with a general reader in mind—anyone who is curious to learn more about a subject and values the knowledge that comes from years of study and academic achievement. The format is what you'd expect to read in many media outlets as well: stories mostly between 800 and 1,200 words long that can be read in a brief amount of time. Since many of the chapters in this collection were originally written in response to events in the news, most have been modified slightly to remove references that would date them. Inevitably, new developments or events will supersede what we published previously, but we have tried to ensure the chapters are accurate.

The themes we have chosen for these collections reflect our editorial values and the makeup of our newsroom. At The Conversation, we have the luxury of having dedicated editors in a wide range of subjects, from education to climate change—something that few media outlets still have the re-sources to do.

Perhaps the biggest payoff from this multidisciplinary approach comes when we examine one subject in depth, as we do in this book. It's enlightening, and often quite fun, to discover what you didn't know by reading an essay from an ethicist, for instance, a few pages after hearing what a micro-biologist or a historian has to say. Having multiple entry points into a subject helps us connect the dots to see the bigger picture. Also, solving thorny societal problems requires a wide-angle view: discussions about new technologies and scientific developments, for example, cannot be separated from the societal impacts they have, just as, say, dealing with environmental challenges requires input from the physical sciences, politics, sociology, and more.

It's worth noting that the multiple voices and different viewpoints in this collection are just that—varied. That means the tone of chapters will vary, and some authors may not even agree on certain points. But that's OK, because the goal is to give you, the reader, the context and a foundational under-standing of issues that are important to living in today's society.

Our hope is that, after reading this collection, you will feel better equipped to make sense of news in the headlines or to grasp the significance of new research. In other cases, you may just be entertained by a good story.

Martin LaMonica

Dispatches from Arkansas

IN APRIL 2021, Arkansas became the first US state to ban gender-affirming health care for trans youth. Overriding a veto by conservative Governor Asa Hutchinson, who described the law as "vast government overreach," the legislature's Saving Adolescents from Experimentation (SAFE) Act not only prohibited anyone under 18 years old from accessing transition-related health care but also barred doctors from providing patients with out-of-state referrals, threatening them with the loss of their licenses or civil lawsuits.[1] As part of a tidal wave of more than 100 pieces of legislation forwarded in over 30 states that spring, the Arkansas law marked a precipitous intensification of anti-trans moral panic.[2] In many ways, this might appear like a conventional American narrative of human rights progress: a moment of cultural recognition is followed by moral panic and political backlash, leaving us to hope that the arc of history will ultimately bend toward justice.

In truth, however, states like Arkansas are participating in a much broader phenomenon of anti-trans politics tied to authoritarian movements. Conservative evangelicals and white supremacist groups in the United States are increasingly allied with anti-trans feminists on the United Kingdom left,[3] but their shared political goals in targeting trans and nonbinary youth also converge with anti-democratic and openly fascist movements in many other places in the world. European human rights organizations have linked the intense turn against trans people in the United Kingdom to far-right scapegoating of LGBT people and the clawback of human rights in Poland and Hungary.[4] Anti-trans rhetoric, which sometimes spills over into violence, has also become a central feature of anti-democratic politicians in Brazil, the Philippines, and Russia.[5] Some of the anti-trans legislation being considered in US states is directly comparable to recent Russian bills, while American right-wing pundits like Tucker Carlson, who frequently platforms anti-trans moral panics, are cozying up to Hungary's far-right.[6]

In sum, not only has it become open season on trans youth in the United States, but the coordinated assault on children and their families also joins a global turn toward strongman politics, the suspension of human rights, and the weakening of democratic norms. Anti-trans politics are hardly a singular wedge issue, a symbolic culture war, or a threat only to trans people themselves. On the contrary, the attack on trans adults and children illuminates much broader and global struggles over basic freedoms and rights.

In Arkansas, the American Civil Liberties Union immediately filed suit against the SAFE Act, and in an initial victory, a federal court temporarily halted the law from taking effect pending the legal challenge's outcome.[7] Yet the fallout from months of anti-trans politicking and the uncertainty over the law's future still hit trans youth hard. "I felt like my life was being signed away," said Sabrina, a teenaged girl who could no longer count on being able to see a doctor and having access to transition-related care. She joined the ACLU suit as a plaintiff, figuring that "if it's not me, it's going to be someone else" and, worse, "if it's not someone else, it's going to be nobody."[8]

Increasingly, this is one kind of trans childhood in the United States, one spent traveling year after year to state capitols, organizing relentlessly to oppose each new legislative attack, and facing the never-ending wear of having to plead for basic rights over and over.[9] While some families of trans youth decided to leave Arkansas in the wake of the bill's passage, for many more who weren't wealthy, objection through mobility simply was not an option. For Zara, a Black trans girl whose family has deep roots in the South, the sentimentalized stories of white trans youth centered in the media left her feeling even less optimistic. If those white kids who at least benefited from the American culture of white innocence faced such an uphill battle, "what hope do we have for Black trans kids?" she wondered.[10]

How is it that trans youth like Sabrina and Zara are facing unprecedented legal disenfranchisement and the planned eradication of their access to transition at the same moment that trans people have never been more well represented in culture and media? Why is a meteoric rise in recognition of gender diversity accompanied by an alarming intensification of authoritarian political movements targeting trans people around the world? And why has a post-truth culture of online disinformation and conspiracy theory latched onto fabulated theories that charge trans peoples with the very violence that is then posed against them?[11]

This anthology of writing on gender diversity, trans people, history, and politics assembles a crucial set of dispatches from both the front lines and the deeper context of battles that trans and nonbinary people face. In an era of endless information streams, hot takes, and the monetization of shallow analysis based in anger or resentment politics, the writers in this book take the time to contextualize the high stakes of today's conversations around gender diversity. Of course, no collection could fully match the complexity of these conversations, and there are many differences among the disciplines and perspectives of contributors, some of which challenge one another. As a historian, I have seen how transformative it can be to press against the myopia of presentism and begin to understand gender and its diversity with the grounding of its actual complexity and history. Rather than appearing out of nowhere, or as a phenomenon of the present world, trans life and gender diversity have deep and enduring roots that can reframe how we approach today's struggles and transformations. But make no mistake: the stakes *are* very high, and none more so than for trans and nonbinary children.

Public perception of social "progress" for trans people often takes cultural barometers for granted, assuming that if trans people are on television or winning recognition for their artistry, then they must be well-off materially; in truth, however, the global rise in anti-trans politics and violence threatens to undo any tepid progress made in recent decades. Legal bans on trans health care nullify the slow but growing adoption of a gender-affirmative care model, which promises to end much of the evaluative gatekeeping and rejection of trans people by medical professionals. For nearly a century, the explicit goal of transgender medicine was to limit access to health care as much as possible by disqualifying most trans people for not being "trans enough" according to narrow and unempirical diagnostic criteria.[12] Under a gender-affirming care model, on the contrary, providers are not supposed to evaluate trans people's worthiness so much as facilitate and support their medical transitions.

Even without recent legislative attacks, though, the affirmative care model is little more than a set of ideals, lacking any means of verification or implementation beyond the good will of medical providers. And for trans youth, as I have written elsewhere, it is unclear whether gender-affirming care is even possible under the existing rubric of "developmentally appropriate" intervention that fundamentally imagines children as incapable of knowing themselves or as undeserving of what they want and need.[13] More pressingly, only a tiny fraction of trans and nonbinary people of any age have access to competent and affordable medical care, even in the United States, meaning that the gender-affirming care model is in the aggregate a useless achievement for most trans people. Even in countries with publicly funded health care, the situation is often dire.

The United Kingdom's National Health Service has effectively sabotaged its own gender care provisions through what activists have decried as the engineering of five-year wait times for adults looking to transition, making it de facto impossible.[14] This issue also affects young people. One clinic provisioned specifically to see trans youth in Devon, England, has simply seen no new patients in five years.[15] Protracted wait times for surgeries and draconian requirements for sterilization or psychiatric evaluation before changing identification documents are only just being revised in countries like Germany and Canada, as political battles imperil the reform process.[16]

The cumulative logic of anti-trans political movements— which also dramatize issues like bathroom access, legal identification, and protection from discrimination in housing, employment, education, and public accommodations—stacks up to an attempt to bar trans people from public life. By depriving trans people from childhood onward of access to equal education, lifesaving health care, and public assistance, and by making it impossible to change names and gender markers on identification documents, it becomes nearly impossible for them to participate in public life, work in the formal economy, and secure housing or transition. Trans people are increasingly pushed into the informal economy and underground spaces, which have historically been the only ones in which they could eke out a living, in the face of disproportionate policing, poverty, and diminished health and life expectancy.[17]

These attempts to disenfranchise trans people from public life are often tied to explicitly authoritarian, policing, and carceral-driven initiatives to punish and immiserate them, especially trans women. Anti-trans feminists in the United

Kingdom, for instance, have insisted on maximally endangering and punishing trans women in the prison system, fabulating that trans women deserve such dehumanizing treatment because they would be ontologically—that is, simply by existing—sexual predators.[18] In the outcome, the constellation of anti-trans political movements flourishing around the globe, frequently aligned with anti-immigrant, ethnonationalist, and white supremacist groups, makes use of anti-trans initiatives in order to weaken democratic institutions, expand repressive state power, and embolden strongmen politicians.

This larger political process is one I have described as the state *declaring itself cisgender*, such that it can consolidate power by compelling citizens to align their gender presentation and bodies with the new ideological fabulation of "biological sex" enshrined in law.[19] While the fallout for trans and nonbinary people under the cis state is extreme, non-trans people will also be affected as their gender becomes more tightly regulated and the expansion of police and carceral apparatuses intensifies existing inequities of race and class. The way that anti-trans political initiatives are often tightly wedded to anti-abortion, anti-democracy, and anti-working-class legislative agendas and policies around the world makes clear how much everyone stands to lose when trans and nonbinary people are targeted.

In such a dire situation, what is to be done? And what lessons does the diversity of gender, as told in the pages of this book, offer us all?

Despite finding itself at the eye of a political storm, Arkansas has also been the site of incredible resilience and alternative visions. While the American national imagination often stereotypes the South as exceptionally hostile to LGBT life, the state capital Little Rock is home to House of GG, an activist community and sanctuary founded and led by Black trans women, including Stonewall veteran Miss Major. House of GG provides a refuge and community for trans people in which to heal. But it also endeavors to train the next generation of Black trans women leaders in South.[20] Far from imagining that they do not belong in places like Arkansas, or that the South is irrevocably hostile to Black trans life, House of GG follows Miss Major's famous rallying cry "I'm still here!" over 50 years after the Stonewall riots in 1969.[21] Rather than viewing the events of recent years as a fall from grace, House of GG frames the struggle as ongoing and connected to the injustices and Black freedom movements of the past. Indeed, the American South is home to a vibrant network of Black trans woman–led organizations stretching from Memphis, to Atlanta, to New Orleans and Little Rock. Far from conceding to the narrow framing of trans issues in the media or mainstream political sphere, these organizations have been quietly at work revolutionizing the conditions of Black trans and poor trans people's lives in the region through mutual aid projects centered on housing, collectively paying for medical care, and supporting people recently released from incarceration.[22] As long as *this* version of transgender Arkansas is overlooked, the full story is not being told.

Indeed, as the ACLU prepared in 2022 to deliver oral arguments before the federal district court hearing the challenge to the SAFE Act, a remarkable amicus brief was filed on behalf of 58 trans people from around the United States.

Rejecting the many patently absurd or disingenuous portrayals by the State of Arkansas of trans people as isolated, permanently unhappy, and unable to live meaningful lives or benefit from transition, the brief was unambiguous: this diverse group of trans people of all ages, genders, races, and walks of life knew gender-affirming care to have "both alleviated suffering *and sparked new joy* in their lives."[23] Refusing to concede to the distorting and prejudicial terms set by transphobic legislators, the brief insisted that these trans people "lead both ordinary and extraordinary lives" (3), with each one bearing an inherent value.[24]

While the amici counted many internationally famous actors, artists, and professionals among them, the brief placed their achievements on par with people like Beck Witt Major of Little Rock, who spoke of the profound meaning of caregiving in the trans community over the past 16 years (7). Rejecting outright the fabrication that trans youth and their transitions are new or unprecedented matters, his partner, Miss Major, who is now in her seventies, explained that she had accessed hormones at the age of 16 (10). Her testimony, as a community leader and member of an elder generation, sat directly alongside that of young people who are now imperiled by laws like Arkansas's.

This trans-generational compact was important in its connection across age groups and its declaration that trans youth are rightly loved, cared for, and supported by *trans* elders, not only families of origin. Speaking through a composite voice, the amicus brief broke through many of the limiting, dramatic tropes of justifying transition in the starkest terms as lifesaving, adding that for many, "gender-affirming care has become an unremarkable part of life" (16). Demonstrating the importance of being allowed to grow up, to age, and to grow old so that transition becomes one day unremarkable, the adults intervening in this case were able to enact a noteworthy form of solidarity with the youth of Arkansas who were facing that opportunity being made illegal. The brief ends with the words of Cecilia Gentili, a longtime advocate and activist: "Transgender youth know who they are, and they know what they need. Our job is to listen to them" (22).

Against the calculated divisiveness that works to keep trans kids and adults separate, or mainly amplifies white, middle-class trans people over trans people of color and poor trans people, the amicus brief further complicates the story from Arkansas with a collective voice. And while Gentili insists on the profound duty to listen to trans youth, she also models listening as the route to active practices of solidarity by adults who care for and support children. This, perhaps, is the most important lesson to take away from the many activists and allies working on the ground today in the struggle against anti-trans political violence, but it is also a lesson to take away from this book. Reading, listening, and learning have become watchwords of gender diversity and inclusion in recent years, but too easily they appear as the beginning and end of the process. The research, stories, and recommendations held in the pages of this book are a rich source for anyone interested in a deeper understanding that can lead to concrete action.

At the beginning of the book's five parts, each one organized around a theme, I offer an introduction that frames the theme: transgender history, the gender binary, gender-nonconforming youth, trans medicine, and human rights and justice. Together with this preface, these part introductions form a long essay arc that travels with you, the reader. This book is not meant to be read and then put away. To read and to listen is to be called to action, to translate learning into active practices of solidarity and organizing.

When trans people, especially trans women and children, find themselves in the crosshairs of a wide constellation of authoritarian, ethnonationalist, and illiberal movements around the globe, an equally broad coalition of progressive people is needed to meet that challenge and stake a claim to a capacious vision of gender freedom and collective self-determination. The time has come to abandon playing defense, only ever reacting to, or trying to mitigate, the worst damage of anti-trans violence. Together, building diverse alliances of the kind that House of GG or the amici intervening in Arkansas have modeled is the call of this moment and the future it so urgently demands.

Notes

1. Asa Hutchinson, "Why I Vetoed My Party's Bill Restricting Health Care for Transgender Youth," *Washington Post*, April 8, 2021, https://www .washingtonpost.com/opinions/asa-hutchinson-veto-transgender -health-bill-youth/2021/04/08/990c43f4-9892-11eb-962b- 78c1d8228819_story.html.
2. Sam Levin, "Mapping Anti-trans Laws Sweeping America: 'A War on 100 Fronts,'" *Guardian*, June 14, 2021, https://www.theguardian.com/society /2021/jun/14/anti-trans-laws-us-map.
3. Cassie Miller, "White Nationalist Threats against Transgender People Are Escalating," Southern Poverty Law Center, June 26, 2019, https://www .splcenter.org/hatewatch/2019/06/26/white-nationalist-threats-against -transgender-people-are-escalating.
4. "Council of Europe Condemns 'Virulent Attacks on LGBT Rights' in the UK, Hungary, and Poland," iNews, January 25, 2022, https://inews .co.uk/news/world/council-of-europe-condemns-virulent-attacks-on

-lgbt-rights-uk-1423399; Scott Neuman, "Local Governments in Poland Rescind Anti-LGBT Resolutions, Fearing Loss of EU Funding," NPR, September 28, 2021, https://www.npr.org/2021/09/28/1041112133 /poland-anti-lgbt-resolutions-eu; Zack Beauchamp, "How Hatred of Gay People Became a Key Plank in Hungary's Authoritarian Turn," Vox, June 28, 2021, https://www.vox.com/22547228/hungary-orban-lgbt-law -pedophilia-authoritarian.

5. Jennifer Ann Thomas, "Threats against Trans Councilwoman Stir Violence Fears in Brazil," Reuters, February 5, 2021, https://www.reuters.com /article/us-brazil-lgbt-rights-trfn/threats-against-trans-councilwomen -stir-violence-fears-in-brazil-idUSKBN2A52EF; "Philippines President Pardons US Marine in Transgender Killing," France 24, July 9, 2020, https://www.france24.com/en/20200907-philippines-president -pardons-us-marine-in-transgender-killing; Maite Fernandez Simon, "'A Woman Is a Woman, a Man Is a Man': Putin Compares Gender Non-conformity to the Coronavirus Pandemic," *Washington Post*, December 23, 2021, https://www.washingtonpost.com/world/2021/12/23/putin -gender-russia-news-conference/.

6. Kaela Roeder, "Russia Lawmakers to Consider Anti-transgender Bill," *Washington Blade*, July 20, 2020, https://www.washingtonblade.com /2020/07/20/russia-lawmakers-to-consider-anti-transgender-bill/; Viktoria Serdult, "Tucker Carlson Has Become Obsessed with Hungary. Here's What He Doesn't Understand," Politico, January 2, 2022, https:// www.politico.com/news/magazine/2022/02/01/tucker-carlson -hungary-orban-00004149.

7. Libby Cathey, "Judge Blocks Arkansas Law Banning Health Care for Transgender Youth," ABC News, July 21, 2021, https://abcnews.go.com /Politics/judge-blocks-arkansas-law-banning-health-care-transgender /story?id=78954056.

8. Sabrina Imbler, "In Arkansas, Trans Teens Await an Uncertain Future," *New York Times*, January 18, 2022, sec. Health, https://www.nytimes .com/2022/01/18/health/transgender-adolescents-arkansas.html.

9. Melissa Gira Grant, "Behind the GOP Strategy to Outlaw Trans Youth," *New Republic*, August 9, 2021, https://newrepublic.com/article/163113 /behind-gop-strategy-outlaw-trans-youth.

10. Imbler, "In Arkansas."

11. I have written more extensively about this dynamic. See Jules Gill-Peterson, "From Gender Critical to QAnon: Anti-trans Politics and the Laundering of Conspiracy," *New Inquiry*, September 13, 2021, https:// thenewinquiry.com/from-gender-critical-to-qanon-anti-trans-politics -and-the-laundering-of-conspiracy/.

12. See Joanne Meyerowitz, *How Sex Changed: A History of Transsexuality in the US* (Cambridge, MA: Harvard University Press, 2004).

13. Jules Gill-Peterson, "On the Possibility of Affirmative Healthcare for

Transgender Children," in Martin Halliwell and Sophie Jones, eds., *The Edinburgh Companion to the Politics of American Health* (Edinburgh: Edinburgh University Press, 2022), chap. 14.

14. "Transgender People Face NHS Waiting List 'Hell,'" BBC, January 9, 2020, https://www.bbc.com/news/uk-england-51006264.

15. Jasmine Anderson, "Devon Gender Clinic Has Not Seen Any New Patients for Five Years, Sparking Search for New Providers," iNews, November 13, 2021, https://inews.co.uk/news/devon-gender-clinic-new-patients-five-years-1299565.

16. Kate Brady, "LGBTQ+ Rights: Germany Appoints First 'Commissioner for Queer Affairs,'" DW, January 6, 2022, https://www.dw.com/en/lgbtq-rights-germany-appoints-first-commissioner-for-queer-affairs/a-60351173; Christine Hauser, "Canada Bans 'Conversion Therapy,'" *New York Times*, January 6, 2022, https://www.nytimes.com/2022/01/06/world/canada/canada-conversion-therapy-law.html.

17. See Susan Stryker, *Transgender History: The Roots of Today's Revolution*, 2nd. ed. (Boston: Seal Press, 2017).

18. Mary Harrington, "How Could the Lords Vote to Let Trans Women in Female Prisons after This Fiasco?," *Daily Mail*, January 15, 2022, https://www.dailymail.co.uk/debate/article-10406427/MARY-HARRINGTON-Lords-vote-let-trans-women-female-prisons-fiasco.html.

19. Jules Gill-Peterson, "The Cis State," *Sad Brown Girl* (blog), April 14, 2021, https://sadbrowngirl.substack.com/p/the-cis-state.

20. "About," House of GG, accessed February 2, 2022, https://houseofgg.org/about/.

21. Lucy Diavolo, "Miss Major Griffin-Gracy Is Still Here and Wants Young

22. Activists to 'Keep on Fighting,'" *Teen Vogue*, June 17, 2020, https://www.teenvogue.com/story/miss-major-griffin-gracy-still-here-young-activists-keep-fighting.

23. Raquel Willis, "Across the South, a Trans Housing Movement Grows," *Vogue*, July 8, 2021, https://www.vogue.com/article/across-the-south-a-trans-housing-movement-grows.

24. Brandt v. Arkansas, Brief of Elliot Page, Major Griffin-Gracy, Gwendolin Herzig, Jazz Jennings, and Fifty-Four Others as Amici Curiae in Support of Plaintiffs-Appellees, United States District Court for the Eastern District of Arkansas, January 20, 2022, p. 2, https://www.clearygottlieb.com/-/media/files/brandt-v-rutledge-amicus-brief.pdf. Page numbers for subsequent references to this document appear parenthetically in-text.

The Conversation on Gender Diversity

Part I.

Lessons from Transgender History

In 2014 *Time* magazine featured actress and activist Laverne Cox on its cover, announcing what it called "the transgender tipping point." The cover story presented a conventional American progress narrative, where civil rights and political representation are seen to follow on the heels of cultural representation. The idea of the tipping point was that trans people had finally arrived to be recognized by the public. If Cox, an outspoken Black trans woman, was making it as an actress in a way once unheard of, then trans people could no longer be ignored by other mainstream institutions. The arrival of trans people was made to seem in this narrative almost predestined to follow other civil rights struggles, especially those for Black freedom and gay marriage. The cover story suggested with an unbridled optimism that something unprecedented and important was on the cusp of taking place for trans people and the society in which they lived.[1]

The many problems with the tipping point's line of reasoning have been carefully dissected by trans commentators and activists, especially Black trans women themselves—including Cox. Its streamlined narrative of US civil rights progress imagines that there is an irrepressible direction of inclusion and emancipation that follows an unshakable script. But by analogizing trans people's human rights to gay people or to African Americans, two specific problems immediately arise. First, we are led to think that the struggle for Black freedom is somehow over or that the fight for gay marriage was separate from the struggles of trans people (when in reality many gay activist organizations actively shunned and excluded trans issues for years). Second, by separating out minority groups in this way, the tipping point fails to acknowledge the rather basic point that some people are Black, gay, *and* transgender. How would those people separate the components of their flesh and blood to fit this succession narrative?

Perhaps most troublingly, the historical narrative of the tipping point has reinforced a kind of collective amnesia about trans people, making them more vulnerable than ever. *Time* joined—and spurred—a chorus of cultural commentators who mistook *their* lack of prior knowledge to be a truthful observation about trans people's existence. In the tipping point narrative, trans people *themselves* are cast as new, as if they have only just arrived on the scene and have no history. Without a widely recognized history, it is easy to question trans people's legitimacy.[2]

Studying trans history offers an urgent correction to the tendency to romanticize or dismiss trans people as generationally new. Indeed, one of the most important critical reactions to the idea of the tipping point has been to historicize it. Instead of reflecting an inevitable march of American progress, the tipping point and its broader cultural milieu have coincided with increased danger for many trans people. The tipping point narrative has reinforced the cultural *hyper*visibility of certain kinds of trans people, especially trans women, putting them at unprecedented risk, rather than granting them respect. The intense interest of mass culture in trans women, children, and trans people of color has not actually resulted in political representation or civil rights protections. On the contrary, scholars and activists alike have pointed out that cultural hypervisibility coincides with a startling backlash that runs the gamut from extremist antitrans laws to escalating rates of violent assault and murder.[3]

To study trans history, then, is never just an intellectual endeavor of curiosity. History plays a signal role in debunking and defending against the shallow, untrue presentism that circulates around trans people. This may be the first time for many to realize that they share the world with trans people, but that does not mean there were no trans people around until recently. Nor does it mean that learning to see trans people in the world is an innocent process.

The charge that being trans or nonbinary is recent is countered by historians with the long, rich, and complex history of gender diversity. Considering how recent terms like *transgender* are—it came into broad usage only in the 1990s—how do we trace the outlines of trans history?[4] In fact, the history of gender diversity begins to dismantle the very categories of today's conversation that are otherwise taken for granted. Not only is there substantial evidence of people who lived differently from the gender they were culturally assigned over the past several centuries and all over the world, regardless of whether they used *trans* words to label themselves. But just as significantly, the ways that trans people have made lives for themselves in the past also challenge us to realize that gender itself is not as stable a social category as we might conventionally expect. The articles in part I are an excellent introduction to some of the most compelling and challenging histories of gender diversity. Think of them as a starting point—a portal to diving deeper into the array of work that historians are undertaking.

It may feel surprising to learn, for instance, that the basic idea of the sex binary—the division of the human species into male and female—is not a very old one. Or that the distinction between sex and gender as many people use it today—including many of the contributors to this book—is barely older than color television. What's more, the root ideas that sex and gender are stable, binary, and self-evident categories of description, from which trans, nonbinary, or intersex people differ, is the result of a long, extremely violent history. The gender binary, in other words, wasn't just invented. It was *imposed* by force on many who did not subscribe to it.

Indigenous historians and historians of the Global South have produced an impressive body of work that tracks the gender binary as an outcome of five centuries of European colonial expansion. In countless cases, European explorers, militaries, and Christian missionaries justified their brutal attacks on Indigenous sovereignty, theft of land, and genocidal violence by describing the people they aggressed as improperly gendered.[5] In other words, gender diversity was a central alibi of colonialism. In 1513, a Spanish expedition in the Caribbean led by Vasco Núñez de Balboa massacred the political leadership of an Indigenous society the Spaniards called the Quarequa. The chronicler attached to the expedition claimed, as justification, that "the village of Quarequa was stained by the foulest vice. The king's brother and a number of other courtiers were dressed as women."[6] Balboa ordered these people (today sometimes called "two spirit") to be rounded up and fed, alive, to dogs the Spanish had bred to be weapons.

Such gender violence of colonialism has been studied not just in the case of the Spanish but the British, French, Germans, and Americans as well. The British colonial administration in India, for instance, attempted to eradicate *hijras* in the late nineteenth century.[7] European colonial powers frequently cast sub-Saharan African women as improperly sexed so as to justify dehumanizing treatment. This process of gendered dehumanization was continuous with slavery in the Americas.[8] And when white plantation owners overthrew the Kingdom of Hawai'i in the 1890s, they justified themselves as securing the islands from the gender and sexual immorality they ascribed to Indigenous Hawaiians.[9]

Yet even in European and American history, the idea that sex can be divided into a clear binary was not popular until well into the twentieth century. The medieval and early modern eras were characterized by many gender-bending stories of miraculous changes of sex.[10] And much Christian iconography and storytelling employed outright nonbinary concepts, centuries before the word was coined.[11] Until the eighteenth century, the Western sciences employed a "one sex" model in which male and female were seen as different expressions of a single biology.[12] In the nineteenth century that idea was overwhelmed by data from studies of evolutionary diversity in the natural world, as well as the new disciplines of embryology and endocrinology. The description of the endocrine system and hormones radically *undermined* any notion that humans were preprogrammed biologically to be exclusively male or female. For one thing, every individual had different endogenous levels of both testosterone and estrogen. And neither genetics, nor chromosomes, nor internal or external organs seemed to predict whether an individual felt like a man or a woman, or something else.

Well into the twentieth century, the dominant scientific paradigm considered sex not to be binary but rather *bisexual*—a word that carried a very different meaning than it does today. Scientists and medical clinicians treated the human species as naturally capable, from the fetal stage, of becoming male, female, or a combination of both.[13] While the science of human development imagined that most people grew over the course of childhood to resemble men or women by adulthood, scientists nevertheless considered everyone naturally to be a mix of both. And the idea that human beings might therefore "change" their sex from one category to another was seen as rather obvious, if rare. Even a scientist as accomplished as Charles Darwin felt that if plants and animals frequently changed sex under the right environmental conditions, it was no stretch to imagine that humans were capable of the same.[14]

Finally, the history of the gender binary contends with the fact that the term *gender* as we conventionally use it in the English language today was not invented until astonishingly recently. While the concept of gender is sometimes associated with trans people, as well as with feminists, it was invented by medical researchers in the 1950s. The psychologist John Money, working with clinical endocrinologists at Johns Hopkins Hospital in Baltimore, defined the term *gender* in a series of research papers in 1955. They needed a concept like gender to satisfy the brutal demands of corrective medicine practiced on intersex people, rather than to expand notions of human diversity. The unit they worked on at Hopkins was dedicated at the time to figuring out how to force children born without typically male or female bodies to accept a binary assignment to one sex or the other. The problem was that neither science, medicine, nor psychology could explain what made someone male or female, or what would make them into a boy or girl. Although clinicians could use nonconsensual surgeries and hormones to force intersex infants into a body categorized visually as male or female, they couldn't force those children to then identify as boys or girls. This was not for lack of trying. The medical records of children from Hopkins documented horrifying attempts by doctors, psychologists, and social workers to force children by any means necessary to outwardly conform to a gender that they did not even give consent to receive.[15]

Money and his research team invented the term *gender* to distinguish the psychological aspect of sex from the biological body because they had to admit that the two didn't reliably align in every case. In their first paper coining the term, they explain that by "gender role" they meant "all those things that a person says or does to disclose himself or herself as having the status of a boy or man, girl or woman, respectively."[16] Incredibly, the distinction between sex and gender that is often taken for granted today as progressive was not invented by feminists, let alone trans activists. It was invented as a conservative tool of medical violence wielded against intersex children. Only beginning in the 1970s did feminists start to adapt the concept to less harmful ends.[17] But the implications of this history for how we use this terminology today are still left to be addressed.

This long history of the sex and gender binary is an important preface to the trans histories included in this book. By understanding that sex, gender, and the binary are not timeless ideas, whether in Western science, culture, or elsewhere in the world, we can appreciate something that *Time* magazine overlooked in its trans tipping point story. Trans and nonbinary people's diversity is not new, but it is not the exception to the rule, either. Seeing trans history as a rich, complex, and diverse field of experience, rather than a singular experience across time, can bring immense rewards. If there is nothing new about gender diversity—if, on the contrary, diversity is *the* main characteristic of the history of gender—then the work of historians provides a powerful framework for contextualizing *everyone's* gender today. Indeed, as the chapters in part I demonstrate, the reason that trans people have not often been included in historical narrative is not simply that they were deliberately erased or hidden. Sometimes trans people, especially white trans men, were able to blend in and live full lives without being subject to the scrutiny and prejudice of cultural visibility.[18] As important as it is to study the past, one of the complicated lessons of trans history is that the state of the world today is not necessarily more welcoming, or safer, for trans people.

The chapters of part I introduce various groups of well-known and everyday trans people from the eighteenth to twentieth centuries, ranging from two-spirit Indigenous peoples in the Americas, to trans children in the 1930s, to trans people on the early internet of the 1990s. In encountering them, we are invited not just to give up the presentism of the post–tipping point world but also to wonder how many more stories have been forgotten or mistaken because we expected the gender binary to be an enduring feature of human history, when in fact history tells us otherwise.

Notes

1. Katy Steinmetz, "The Transgender Tipping Point," *Time*, May 29, 2014, https://time.com/magazine/us/135460/june-9th-2014-vol-183-no-22-u-s/.
2. For a larger discussion of how trans people are framed as "new," see the introduction to Jules Gill-Peterson, *Histories of the Transgender Child* (Minneapolis: University of Minnesota Press, 2018), 1–35.
3. For wide-ranging coverage of the problem of hypervisibility, see Reina Gossett, Eric A. Stanley, and Johanna Burton, eds., *Trap Door: Trans*

Cultural Production and the Politics of Visibility, illus. ed. (Cambridge, MA: MIT Press, 2017). See also Eric A. Stanley, *Atmospheres of Violence: Structuring Antagonism and the Trans/Queer Ungovernable* (Durham, NC: Duke University Press, 2021).

4. On the emergence of the term *transgender* in the 1990s, see David Valentine, *Imagining Transgender: An Ethnography of a Category*, illus. ed. (Durham, NC: Duke University Press, 2007).

5. On this vast subject, there are a number of excellent starting points for interested readers. See especially Qwo-Li Driskill, *Asegi Stories: Cherokee Queer and Two-Spirit Memory* (Tucson: University of Arizona Press, 2016); and Deborah A. Miranda (Ohlone-Costanoan Esselen Nation, Chumash), "Extermination of the *Joyas*: Gendercide in Spanish California," *GLQ: A Journal of Lesbian and Gay Studies* 16, no. 1 (2010): 253–84. See also Zeb Tortorici, *Sins against Nature: Sex and Archives in Colonial New Spain* (Durham, NC: Duke University Press, 2018); Walter L. L. Williams, *Spirit and the Flesh: Sexual Diversity in American Indian Culture* (Boston: Beacon Press, 1992); and Evan B. Towle and Lynn Marie Morgan, "Romancing the Transgender Native: Rethinking the Use of the 'Third Gender' Concept," *GLQ: A Journal of Lesbian and Gay Studies* 8, no. 4 (2002): 469–97.

6. Francis Augustus MacNutt, *De Orbo Novo: The Eight Decades of Peter Martyr D'Anghera*, vol. 1 (G. P. Putnam and Sons, 1912), 284–85.

7. Jessica Hinchy, *Governing Gender and Sexuality in Colonial India: The Hijra, c. 1850–1900* (Cambridge: Cambridge University Press, 2019).

8. Jennifer L. Morgan, *Laboring Women: Reproduction and Gender in New World Slavery* (Philadelphia: University of Pennsylvania Press, 2004).

9. J. Kehaulani Kauanui, *Paradoxes of Hawaiian Sovereignty: Land, Sex, and the Colonial Politics of State Nationalism* (Durham, NC: Duke University Press Books, 2018).

10. An excellent overview of this era from a range of scholarly perspectives can be found in Greta LaFleur, Masha Raskolnikov, and Anna Klosowska, eds., *Trans Historical: Gender Plurality before the Modern* (Ithaca, NY: Cornell University Press, 2021).

11. See Leah DeVun, *The Shape of Sex: Nonbinary Gender from Genesis to the Renaissance* (New York: Columbia University Press, 2021).

12. Thomas Laqueur, *Making Sex: Body and Gender from the Greeks to Freud* (Cambridge, MA: Harvard University Press, 1992).

13. See Gill-Peterson, *Histories of the Transgender Child*, 35–58.

14. Charles Darwin, *The Variation of Plants and Animals under Domestication* (New York: Appleton, 1896), 26.

15. See Gill-Peterson, *Histories the Transgender Child*, 97–128.

16. John Money, "Hermaphroditism, Gender and Precocity in Hypernadrenocorticism: Psychologic Findings," *Bulletin of the Johns Hopkins Hospital* 96, no. 6 (1955): 253–64, 258.

17. Jennifer Germon, *Gender: A Genealogy of an Idea* (New York: Palgrave Macmillan, 2009).

18. See Emily Skidmore, *True Sex: The Lives of Trans Men at the Turn of the Twentieth Century* (rpt., New York: New York University Press, 2019); and Jen Manion, *Female Husbands* (Cambridge: Cambridge University Press, 2021).

Chapter 1

Forgotten Figures Who Challenged Gender Expression and Identity Centuries Ago

CATHERINE ARMSTRONG

NONBINARY AND TRANS PEOPLE have always been here, in every recorded society from the ancient world onward. Why is it then that they're often absent from the tales and lists of historical figures we hear about? The answer lies, in part, with how history is recorded and who records it.

People who belong to groups that fear being ostracized and persecuted often only reveal their true selves to a few people. As a result, the visibility of LGBT+ people, even during moments in history when they have faced open hostility, is often limited. Coupled with that is a dearth of historical records because authors of these historical accounts were often prejudiced and did not want to record the experiences of those considered shameful under the values of their time.

Historians working on the queer past need to understand why LGBT+ people, along with members of other marginalized groups, don't appear as often in recorded history compared with those outside these communities. Fortunately, historians are now beginning to look around more carefully to find these important stories.

Gender Presentation
in the 18th and 19th Centuries

Our understanding of being transgender has evolved considerably in the last few decades. Transgender experiences aren't necessarily limited to people who undergo medical procedures to alter their body; they also include people who present themselves as different from the gender they were assigned at birth.

Much of society now appreciates that the gender to which a person is assigned at birth might be entirely different from their gender identity, which is different again from their gender expression. On one level, a person's gender is defined by how they identify, that is, how they feel internally: as a woman, as a man, as neither, or as anything in between on the gender spectrum. But what is also important is your gender expression, that is, the deliberate and accidental signals you give to others about your gender through aspects such as what you wear and how you cut your hair.

Although the terminology we use to describe gender would have been alien in the 18th and early 19th centuries, many people living in those eras would have understood the concepts. Some women who were sexually and romantically attracted to other women, then as now, presented as more masculine, both for personal gratification and sometimes to be accepted by society.

Anne Lister (or "Gentleman Jack"—the subject of a BBC television series starring Suranne Jones) is a good example. Under 19th-century ideas of gender, she would have been perceived by others as masculine, and it wasn't until 1988, when the biographer Helena Whitbread decoded her diaries, that the true extent of her lesbian relationships and life was discovered.[1]

Other women presented themselves as men for reasons of career ambition because they wished to make life choices denied to the half of the population assigned female at birth. In the American Civil War, Franklin Thompson and Harry Buford were widely praised soldiers who fought for and spied for the Confederate states. Both were women passing as men, or in the phrase of historian Matthew Teorey, who has studied their lives, women who "unsexed" themselves.[2]

An earlier example of gender fluidity is the 18th-century case of the Chevalier D'Eon,[3] who worked for French king Louis XV as a spy in London before later claiming political exile in England. The Chevalier became a minor society celebrity and presented as a man and a woman at various points in their life, until around age 50, when they began to live permanently as a woman.

Being Transgender in a Global Context

It is important to understand that the lives of LGBT+ people in the past were experienced very differently in cultures outside Europe. The notion of a third gender, or *Māhū*, is part of Polynesian culture.[4] It can mean a gender between male and female or mean gender-fluid. In Hawai'i and Tahiti, *Māhū* people were highly respected in native culture as keepers of oral traditions and historical knowledge. They often taught the hula dance, famous to the region, which has a leisure function but also an important spiritual meaning. *Māhū* people existed not only in the past but are an important part of queer culture in Hawai'i today.

Other native cultures also display a deep respect for gender diversity. The Navajo tribe from the southwestern United States have a gender category called *Nádleehi*, which can refer to transgender people who have transitioned in one direction along the gender binary (having been assigned male at birth and now identifying as female, or assigned female at birth and now identifying as male), to gender-fluid people, and to those whose gender presentation is more masculine or feminine than their gender identity suggests. *Nádleehi* in Navajo culture have a spiritual function as well as being respected tribal members in their own right.[5]

Compared with Western societies, this difference in perception was noted by anthropologists as early as the 1920s. Author William Willard Hill was surprised that Navajo society considered a transgender person "very fortunate," unlike in his own culture in the United States, where gender fluidity caused anxiety in mainstream society.[6] Such is a timely reminder that it's always important to look outside one's own culture to learn about inclusion and diversity. You might be surprised by what you discover.

Notes

1. "Anne's Story," Anne Lister, n.d., https://www.annelister.co.uk/.
2. Matthew Teorey, "Unmasking the Gentleman Soldier in the Memoirs of Two Cross-Dressing Female US Civil War Soldiers," *War, Literature, and the Arts: An International Journal of the Humanities* 20 (2008): 74-93.
3. "The Chevalier d'Eon," British Museum, n.d., https://www.britishmuseum.org/collection/desire-love-and-identity/chevalier-deon.
4. Eleisha Lauria, "Gender Fluidity in Hawaiian Culture," *Gay & Lesbian Review Worldwide* 24, no. 1 (2017): 31-33.
5. Carolyn Epple, "Coming to Terms with Navajo Nádleehí: A Critique of Berdache, 'Gay,' 'Alternate Gender,' and Two-Spirit.'" *American Ethnologist* 25, no. 2 (1998): 267-90.
6. Epple, "Coming to Terms."

Chapter 2

Trans Kids in the US Were Seeking Treatment Decades before Today's Political Battles over Access to Health Care

JULES GILL-PETERSON

IN 1942, a 17-year-old transgender girl named Lane visited a doctor in her Missouri hometown with her parents. Lane had known that she was a girl from a very young age, but fights with her parents over her transness had made it difficult for her to live comfortably and openly during her childhood. She had dropped out of high school and was determined to get out of Missouri as soon as she was old enough to pursue a career as a dancer.

The doctor reportedly found "a large portion of circulating female hormone" in her body during his examination and suggested to Lane's parents that he undertake an exploratory laparotomy—a surgery in which he would probe her internal organs to find out more about her endocrine system.[1] But the appointment ended abruptly after her father refused the surgery, objecting that "the doctor did not know what he was talking about."

I first encountered Lane's story buried among the papers of an endocrinologist. Her brief encounter with a doctor during her teenage years was typical of many transgender children like her in the early to mid-20th century. These stories form a key thread of the first several chapters of my book *Histories of the Transgender Child*,[2] and they point to the tremendous obstacles these kids faced in a world where the word *transgender* didn't even exist.

The Living Laboratories of Gender

In the first half of the 20th century, there was nothing like today's gender-affirming pediatric care model, which involves building a social support network and can include treatments such as hormone blockers.[3] Doctors simply did not allow trans patients to transition.

That doesn't mean doctors and researchers weren't interested in seeing children like Lane as patients. But instead of supporting their wishes and hopes, doctors tended to see them as canvases for experimentation—to see how their growing bodies responded to various surgeries or hormonal cocktails. In my research I tracked several decades of this kind of medical research, beginning in the early 20th century at research hospitals such as Johns Hopkins Hospital in Baltimore.

In fact, medical researchers were particularly interested in treating still-developing LGBTQ youths as a way to refine their techniques for forcing intersex children into one of a binary of sexes,[4] or for carrying out conversion therapy, which aimed to coerce gay children into a heterosexual outcome and gender-confirming behavior.

In this climate, Lane's father may have unwittingly saved her from a harmful attempt at "corrective" surgery or hormones to try to prevent her from being trans. Even though Lane left home at age 18 to live as a woman, she would have to wait over a decade before finally obtaining access to hormones and surgery in the mid-1950s.

Trans Childhoods before Trans Medicine

The struggles of trans children in the era before modern transgender medicine show not just how trans youths are far from a new phenomenon but also how tenacious and forward-thinking they were compared with their parents and doctors.

Two stories of other trans people like Lane show how clinicians' refusal to let them transition never stopped them from being trans. Both of them found their way to the Johns Hopkins Hospital, which, during the first seven decades of the 20th century, was widely regarded as the premier institution in the United States for people with questions about their sex and gender.

When psychologists at Johns Hopkins interviewed a retired trans woman from the Midwest in 1954, she told them about her childhood in the 1890s. Even then, without any concept or term for being trans, this woman—by then in her sixties—told them it was obvious to her that she was a girl.

"I wanted a doll and buggy very much," she reminisced of her intense attachment to the toys given only to girls. While her wish to be a girl never waned, her life had never afforded her the opportunity to transition to living full-time as a woman until she retired.

Five years later, the clinicians at Johns Hopkins met a trans man who was then in his thirties. He had come to them seeking top and bottom surgery. Growing up in rural upstate New York in the 1930s, he had been forced to drop out of school "because of the excruciating sense of embarrassment at being obliged to wear girls' clothes."

Unlike the trans woman from the Midwest, this trans man, as a teenager, found a path to living openly as a boy: manual labor at a lumber mill. By working in a men's profession and proving his masculinity through showcasing his strength, his presentation as a boy was embraced by his community. Decades later, he sought out the doctors at Hopkins only to confirm what had long been true in his life: that he was a man.

Growing Up despite Every Obstacle

Each of these three children—and countless more from the early 20th century—had to wait until adulthood to finally transition. Yet the failure of doctors and other gatekeepers to stop them from transitioning as children, and their inability to access any form of gender-affirming medical treatment, hardly prevented them from being trans or growing up to be trans adults.

This is all the more remarkable given that, before the

1950s, few Americans had access to any concept or information about trans life. While small communities of adult trans people are evident as far back as the turn of the 20th century,[5] most children would not have had access to these discreet social worlds, which tended to exist in major cities like New York and San Francisco. Without any media to influence them (a purported menace by those who stir moral panic), and without role models, these remarkable young people were able to stay true to their inner feelings en route to living trans lives.

They're a reminder that conversion therapy, attempts to suppress or limit transness, and gatekeeping through legislation don't work.

They didn't work a century ago and they won't work today.

Notes

1. "Exploratory Laparotomy," Saint Luke's Health System, n.d., https://www.saintlukeskc.org/health-library/exploratory-laparotomy.
2. Jules Gill-Peterson, *Histories of the Transgender Child* (Minneapolis: University of Minnesota Press, 2018).
3. John Rafferty, "Ensuring Comprehensive Care and Support for Transgender and Gender-Diverse Children and Adolescents," in *Pediatric Collections: LGBTQ+: Support and Care (Part 3: Caring for Transgender Children)* (Washington, DC: American Academy of Pediatrics, 2021), 5–18. https://doi.org/10.1542/9781610025423-ensuring.
4. Kimberly Mascott Zieselman, "I Was an Intersex Child Who Had Surgery. Don't Put Other Kids through This," *USA Today*, August 9, 2017, https://www.usatoday.com/story/opinion/2017/08/09/intersex-children-no-surgery-without-consent-zieselman-column/539853001/.
5. Susan Stryker, *Transgender History: The Roots of Today's Revolution*, 2nd. ed. (New York: Seal Press, 2017).

Chapter 3

The Early 20th–Century German Trans-Rights Activist Who Was Decades ahead of His Time

ELIZABETH HEINEMAN

FOR FAR TOO LONG, transgender people have suffered indignities ranging from loved ones' refusal to recognize their gender identity to outright violence and legal discrimination. Those opposed to recognizing gender identity sometimes call it a form of "radical gender ideology" or "political correctness" gone too far.

But recognition of transgender identity is no recent phenomenon. Many cultures have long recognized genders outside the male-female binary. Even in the Western world, some doctors acknowledged gender-nonconforming people far earlier than we often realize. In the medical field, perhaps the most important pioneer was German physician Magnus Hirschfeld, who was born in 1868. As a historian of gender and sexuality in Germany, I'm struck by how he paved the way for the legal recognition of gender-nonconforming people.

Hirschfeld's "Sexual Intermediaries"

In recent years, the medical and psychological professions have come to a consensus that sex assignment at birth is inadequate for understanding individuals' sexual and gender identity—and that failure to recognize this fact can have a devastating impact.

Magnus Hirschfeld was the first doctor to openly research and advocate for people whose gender did not correspond with their sex assignment at birth. He's often remembered today as an advocate of gay rights, and in the early 20th century, his activism played a major role in nearly overturning Germany's law criminalizing male same-sex relations.[1]

But Hirschfeld's vision extended much farther than homosexuality. He defined his specialty as "sexual inter-mediaries," which included everyone who did not fit into an "ideal type" of heterosexual, cisgendered men and women.[2] According to Hirschfeld, sexual intermediaries included many categories. One type was cisgendered people who were gay, lesbian, or bisexual. Another consisted of transvestites: people who comfortably identified as their assigned sex but

Dr. Magnus Hirschfeld. *AP Photo*

who preferred to dress in the clothing assigned to the other sex. Yet others were "trans" in a more radical direction, like those who wanted to live fully as their nonassigned sex or longed for sex-change surgery.

A Relentless Advocate

As a gay man, Hirschfeld was aware of the legal and social dangers that sexual intermediaries faced.[3]

Since sexual intermediaries often turned to their doctors for help, Hirschfeld worked to educate the medical community. He published medical journals including the *Yearbook on Sexual Intermediaries* and the *Journal of Sexual Science*. In 1919 he founded the Institute for Sexual Science in Berlin to promote further research.

He also sought to educate the public. In court he gave expert testimony on behalf of men who had been accused of violating Germany's law banning male same-sex relations. He even cowrote and made a cameo appearance in the world's first feature-length movie featuring a gay protagonist: the 1919 silent film *Anders als die Anderen* (*Different from the Others*).[4] Nor did Hirschfeld shy away from political engagement. In 1897 he founded the Scientific Humanitarian Committee to advocate for gender and sexual rights.

Then, from 1897 to 1898, Hirschfeld worked to decriminalize male same-sex relations in Germany. He collected over 5,000 signatures from Germans willing to be publicly identified with the effort, including such luminaries as Albert Einstein and Thomas Mann.[5] A bill decriminalizing male homosexual acts gained only minority support when it was introduced in Parliament in 1898, but a new bill was reintroduced after the First World War. In the more progressive environment of the Weimar Republic,[6] the bill advanced to parliamentary committee, only to stall when the Great Depression hit in 1929.

Importantly, Hirschfeld's advocacy extended well beyond the decriminalization of gay male sex. (Women's same-sex intimacy was socially disparaged but not illegal.)

Like most European countries, Germany had—and still has—an "internal passport," government-issued identification that citizens are expected to carry with them. Germans whose passport indicated "male" but who dressed in female clothing were subject to police harassment or arrest for disorderly conduct. Together with a colleague, Hirschfeld convinced the Berlin police in 1910 to accept a "transvestite certificate," signed by a doctor, to nullify such charges. After the First World War, he convinced the Prussian judiciary to permit legal name changes from gender-specific names to gender-neutral names, which enabled trans people to present as the gender that was true to themselves.

Not all sexual minorities in Germany endorsed Hirschfeld's views. Early 20th-century Germany was a politically and culturally diverse place, and that diversity extended to people attracted to members of the same sex and to gender-nonconforming people. Some gay men, for example, argued that far from being an "intermediary" sexual type, they were the most masculine men of all: after all, they didn't form close bonds with women. The vision of these "masculinists" had little room for lesbians, bisexuals, or trans people.

A Life's Work Goes Up in Flames

By contrast, Hirschfeld's approach was all-inclusive. In his view, all sexual intermediaries—whether L, G, B, T, Q, or I in today's parlance—were worth recognizing and protecting. He once calculated that there were 43,046,721 possible variants of human sexuality. That was simply another way of saying that the human species was infinitely diverse. "Love," he said, "is as varied as people are."[7]

When the Nazis came to power in 1933, Hirschfeld, who was Jewish, was on an international tour lecturing on sexual science. From abroad, he watched newsreels of his Institute for Sexual Science set aflame by Nazi storm troopers. Thousands of unique medical records, publications, photos, and artifacts were destroyed.

Hirschfeld died two years later, and materials confiscated by the Nazis became evidence against gender-nonconforming and sexually nonconforming people in the Third Reich. Male same-sex relations weren't decriminalized in East Germany until 1968 and in West Germany until 1969.[8] Full legal equality had to wait even longer.

Nearly a century after Hirschfeld's institute burned, only tentative progress has been made toward ending discrimination based on gender identity. And that progress is at risk. Yet no bureaucratic definition of *sex* will change what Hirschfeld so clearly demonstrated over 120 years ago: trans people exist. The question that remains is whether we will come to recognize their full human dignity.

Notes

1. Eric Marcus, "Magnus Hirschfeld," *Making Gay History*, podcast audio, October 25, 2018, 28:06, https://makinggayhistory.com/podcast/magnus-hirschfeld/.
2. Magnus Hirschfeld, *Berlin's Third Sex*, trans. James J. Conway (1904; Berlin: Rixdorf Editions, 2017).

3. Ralf Dose, *Magnus Hirschfeld and the Origins of the Gay Liberation Movement*, trans. Edward H. Willis (New York: Monthly Review Press, 2014).

4. *Anders als die Andern* (*Different from the Others*) (Weimar Republic: Richard Oswald–Film Berlin, 1919).

5. Elena Mancini, *Magnus Hirschfeld and the Quest for Sexual Freedom* (Basingstoke, UK: Palgrave Macmillan, 2015).

6. Robert Beachy, *Gay Berlin: Birthplace of a Modern Identity* (New York: Vintage Books, 2015); Laurie Marhoefer, *Sex and the Weimar Republic: German Homosexual Emancipation and the Rise of the Nazis* (Toronto: University of Toronto Press, 2015).

7. Edward Ross Dickinson, *Sex, Freedom, and Power in Imperial Germany, 1880–1914* (New York: Cambridge University Press, 2014), 159.

8. Clayton J. Whisnant, *Male Homosexuality in West Germany: Between Persecution and Freedom 1945–69* (Basingstoke, UK: Palgrave Macmillan, 2012).

Chapter 4

How the Bulletin Board Systems, Email Lists, and GeoCities Pages of the Early Internet Created a Place for Trans Youth to Find One Another and Explore Coming Out

AVERY DAME-GRIFF

FOLLOW COVERAGE OF TRANS ISSUES, and you'll hear some people say that teens who change their gender identity are participating in a fad and that social media is the culprit. As one proponent of legislation that would restrict access to care for trans teens claimed, social media platforms are where trans youths are falsely "convinced" that their feelings of identifying as a gender other than the one assigned to them at birth—known as gender dysphoria—are valid.

These fears of Instagram, Tumblr and TikTok as breeding grounds for instilling gender dysphoria in young people recall other moral panics over new media, from the Victorian-era paranoia that serialized stories called "penny dreadfuls" were going to incite a youth crime wave to 20th-century anxiety over children's exposure to violence on television.[1] Contemporary fears ignore the long-documented history of trans youth in North America,[2] while assuming that trans youth using social media to find social support and build community is somehow a new phenomenon.

As I've found in my research on early digital trans communities, trans youths have been online since the late 1980s. They weren't seeking out information and community because their friends were all doing it. They were doing it of their own accord.

Trans Adults Hesitant to Engage

For a long time, adults within trans community organizations largely avoided contact with legal minors. Even though many had recognized their own cross-gender feelings from a young age, they feared backlash from parents or law enforcement if they interacted with youths who sought them out.

In a 1996 column, transgender publisher Kymberleigh Richards reported that physician Sheila Kirk, medical adviser to the International Foundation for Gender Education—the largest transgender advocacy organization at the time—said that the organization often had to cut off contact with teens who reached out, since the majority of them didn't have parental consent to communicate with the organization. Richards also wrote that adult members of regional trans support groups feared that angry parents might charge them with "contributing to the delinquency of a minor."[3]

Even Richards, who'd done informal phone counseling with trans youths, felt uncomfortable regularly talking with teens without a referring doctor or nurse on the line. Yet Richards was hopeful that the internet could be a safe space for these youths. Because many of these spaces were anonymous, trans youth could find support and resources by interacting with adults.

Dialing In and Making Connections

Some of the first recorded examples of trans youth exploring trans communities online date back to 1988.

Unlike today's always-on internet, the online landscape of the late 1980s and early 1990s varied widely. Some folks connected with others on bulletin board systems, which were independent computer servers often run out of the system operator's home. Instead of an IP (Internet Protocol) or web address, users would dial in to a specific phone number using their modem. The cost of extended long-distance calls limited users mostly to those living in the bulletin board system's area code. In many ways, these networks were some of the earliest forms of social media. Others used national subscription services like America Online, CompuServe Information Service, Prodigy, or GEnie. Most importantly, whether you used a bulletin board system or a subscription service, you received your own email address.

In CompuServe's trans-specific Genderline forum,[4] in chatrooms, or on CDForum, an early trans email list, trans youths were able to ask questions and learn how to safely explore their cross-gender feelings, find supportive therapists, and grow their social networks.

For example, 17-year-old Susie, a first-generation

Chinese immigrant living in Canada, was a regular poster to CDForum throughout 1992. In her archived emails, available through the Queer Digital History Project, she asked members for advice on managing her depression and kept them updated on major changes in her life. Most of the members Susie and other trans youth communicated with were trans adults, yet once the World Wide Web—and the home page, in particular—took off, spaces by and for trans youth became far more common.

Becoming Visible

Though websites like GeoCities are now something of an internet joke, they were an important place where trans youths could come out and publicly identify as trans.

During the mid-to-late 1990s, ad-supported web hosting services allowed users to create their own websites, or home pages, that featured a variety of personalized content, from hobbies and fandoms to photo collections and journals. Compared with text-heavy bulletin board systems or email lists, homepages were vibrant: most home page creators decorated their spaces as you might your bedroom, using an array of colors, typefaces, embedded music files, and animated graphics as GIFs.

The Transgendered Teens Web Directory, created in 1998 and last archived in 2002, included links, home pages, and email addresses for youths from 32 different states. These home pages contained a variety of information, from advice on coming out and navigating being out in high school, to pursuing medical transition as a teen.

For example, the web diary of Transgendered Teens Web Directory founder Sarah, which has entries from 1997 to 2001, repeatedly references her email chats with other trans youths, who support her while she navigates her shifting identity, coming out to her parents, and making friends.

Trans youths also created resources that focused on what they thought other youths needed. On the TransBoy Resource Network's "About" page, the creator describes being inspired by their own experience with "the potential the internet has for bringing trans people together and for the dissemination of information."

Most importantly, for trans youths who couldn't be themselves in real life, the home page was a space for self-expression. On their pages, they could use gendered colors and graphics without fear of outing themselves or post photos wearing the clothes they felt comfortable in without facing physical harassment. For trans creators who had supportive parents, their home page could even become a place to share their transition progress by posting photos at each new personal milestone.

Much like today's social media profiles, the home page became a digital version of one's ideal self. Over time, the growing number of pages meant that trans youths surfing the web were, as teenager Dylan Jared wrote on his page, always able to "run across people like themselves."

Trans Teens Grow Their Ranks

Through these online spaces, what had once seemed rare—publicly identifying as trans before becoming an adult—was rapidly becoming a common experience for a large part of the trans community.[5]

As trans youths became more visible, organizations felt

empowered to actively advocate on their behalf. Issues facing trans youth were a central theme of the 2004 annual conference of the International Foundation for Gender Education, although some attendees still worried about the ethical issues of having youths give presentations. Throughout the early 2000s, the number of people in North America coming out as trans earlier in life grew exponentially. Now, some trans-affirming clinics struggle to see all their prospective patients.

This shift wouldn't have been possible without the reach of the internet, which showed that trans youth have always been here. Online communities gave them a place—and a space—to be themselves, without fear of being ostracized, undermined, or harassed. And it's having the support of their peers, not a passing social media fad, that's giving them the courage to come out, then and now.

Notes

1. John Springhall, " 'Penny Dreadful' Panic (II): Their Scapegoating for Late-Victorian Juvenile Crime," in *Youth, Popular Culture and Moral Panics: Penny Gaffs to Gangsta-Rap, 1830–1996* (Basingstoke, UK: Palgrave Macmillan, 1999), 71–97.
2. Jules Gill-Peterson, "Transgender Childhood Is Not a 'Trend' " *New York Times*, April 5, 2021, https://www.nytimes.com/2021/04/05/opinion /transgender-children.html.
3. Kymberleigh Richards, *Cross-Talk: The Transgender Community News & Information Monthly*, no. 77 (March 1996), https://www.digitaltransgender archive.net/files/vd66vz962.
4. Psychologist Roger E. Peo described teenagers' experiences with Genderline in a column from 1989. "Roger's Notebook (#30): Teenage Crossdressers," *TV-TS Tapestry*, no. 54 (1989): 77, https://archive.org /details/tvtstapestry54unse/page/76/mode/2up.
5. Megan Davidson, "Seeking Refuge under the Umbrella: Inclusion, Exclusion, and Organizing within the Category *Transgender*," *Sexuality Research and Social Policy* 4, no. 4 (2007): 60–80, https://doi.org/10.1525 /srsp.2007.4.4.60.

Chapter 5

Trans People Have a Long History in Appalachia— but Politicians Prefer to Ignore It

G. SAMANTHA ROSENTHAL

IN PUBLIC DEBATE throughout the South, transness—the fact of being transgender—is framed as a kind of new social contagion.

Count me among the afflicted.

When I first moved to Appalachia in 2015, I expected to find a hostile environment for my own transition. Instead, I met trans people of all ages whose stories demonstrate that there is nothing new about being transgender in southwest Virginia. Yet this remarkable history is all but forgotten.

When politicians frame transgender youth as a new phenomenon, they ignore the fact that gender-nonconforming
young people have existed for generations.[1] Without a historical perspective, decisions can be made that negatively impact
young people.

For example, legislation in the South has focused on
prohibiting transgender youths from partaking in a variety of
activities, including school athletics and lifesaving health care.
In southwest Virginia, several county school boards in the
summer of 2021 voted to reject new state guidelines aimed at
providing support for transgender students. And in November
2021, Glenn Youngkin won the Virginia governorship on a
platform of "parents' rights," building on the furor of parents
regarding the state's overreach on curricular matters and
policies regarding trans students.

This ongoing panic over transgender bodies is evidence
of the increasing visibility of transgender people in rural
America. As a trans woman who researches and writes about
transgender history, I know this history well.

Local Transgender Voices

In my book *Living Queer History: Remembrance and Belonging in a Southern City,*[2] I write about Miss Carolyn. She grew
up in rural West Virginia in the 1950s and 1960s. As she tells it:
"I always been Carolyn from 5 all the way up to 67. But I always
been, I always know the way I was." As a teenager, she would
sneak out late at night with a friend, both of them dressed in
women's clothes, and dance sexily down the streets.

But it wasn't until she moved to Roanoke, Virginia, in
1972 that she was able to become her full self. She started

performing on area stages as a drag queen and worked downtown as a sex worker. In an era of desegregation, she became the first Black queen to win the region's premier drag pageant in 1975.

When a college student interviewed her in 2018 about her life, she said some people call her *she*, some call her *he*, and she doesn't mind which you use. She said that the word *transgender* wasn't a thing when she was growing up and coming out, but if she had known what she knows now, she would have claimed *transgender* for herself.

Carolyn was not alone. She mentored several other queens in Roanoke who worked at nightclubs and on the streets.

One of those performers was a young white trans woman named Rhoda, who grew up in Roanoke in the 1950s. While attending college, Rhoda underwent "a battery of psychological tests," as she put it. Ultimately, a doctor at the University of Virginia's Gender Identity Program prescribed her the hormones estrogen and progestin.

By the time she took the stage in Roanoke in 1977, she had visible breasts. She had recently changed her legal identification and was preparing to marry a man and live her life as a woman. "I'm a transsexual—a woman," she told a local magazine in 1977. "Ever since I can remember, that's the way I've felt."[3]

Supporters celebrate transgender protection measures that were voted into the school system's policies at the Loudoun County Public Schools Administration Building on August 11, 2021, in Ashburn, Virginia.
Ricky Carioti / The Washington Post via Getty Images

Outside the world of nightclubs, another white trans woman named Rona was a local activist who, in the 1970s, distributed literature about transgender families to local public libraries.[4] She also made sure local police departments had up-to-date information on transgender people. In 1980, she helped to found the first transgender organization in southwest Virginia, a budding chapter of the national Society for the Second Self, or Tri-Ess. Rona raised the issue of transgender rights in southwest Virginia five decades before local school boards here would return to the issue.

Trans Youth and Trans History

Transgender history has the power to shape contemporary experiences of belonging. For trans youths in rural communities, history can be a tool not just for knowing the past but for reimagining our present. These stories let young people know that they are not alone, that they are not the first to struggle, and that they have a right to be here.

For several years I co-led a workshop with the Southwest Virginia LGBTQ+ History Project at a summer camp for LGBTQ teenagers in the Appalachian Mountains. This workshop, "Living Trans History," asked participants, some of whom were as young as middle school age, to read excerpts from oral histories with trans elders.

After reading the transcripts, the youths were put into small groups and tasked with developing short theatrical performances that brought these elders' stories to life. One group created a skit focused on the role of the church in denouncing gender nonconformity. Another performance centered on a trans woman who found an unlikely home in a rough-and-tumble bar. Another was about a sex worker who worked the streets of Roanoke.

After their performances, we asked the campers to reflect on their experiences with these stories. They highlighted the similarities and differences across the generations and remarked on their new understanding of themselves. They also realized that they were not the first trans people to live in southwest Virginia, a recognition that can foster a renewed sense of meaning and belonging.

If rural transgender history is brought to light, perhaps it will help communities such as mine remember that trans people have always been here.

Transness itself is a reminder of the past—an assigned sex, a given name, a pubescent body. It is difficult for trans people to escape from that history, and it can feel like abuse. Perhaps that's why queer studies scholar Heather Love writes that, for LGBTQ people, "the challenge is to engage with the past without being destroyed by it."[5]

Trans youths experience the abuse of having their own personal histories used against them by school administrators and sometimes by their own parents. But they deserve to know a richer archive than just what's printed on their birth certificates. Trans history has the power to transform. It gives communities the tools they need for making safer spaces for all.

Notes

1. Jules Gill-Peterson, *Histories of the Transgender Child* (Minneapolis: University of Minnesota Press, 2018).
2. G. Samantha Rosenthal, *Living Queer History: Remembrance and Belonging in a Southern City* (Chapel Hill: University of North Carolina Press, 2021).
3. Stefan Bechtel, "The Long Road from Man to Woman," *Roanoker* 4, no. 6 (December 1977): 25–69.
4. Virginia Prince Charles, *The Transvestite and His Wife: A Discussion from Both Points of View* (Los Angeles: Chevalier Publications, 1967).
5. Heather Love, *Feeling Backward: Loss and the Politics of Queer History* (Cambridge, MA: Harvard University Press, 2009).

Part II.

**Cultural Change and
the Gender Binary**

Many primers on trans and nonbinary issues focus overwhelmingly on identity: what it means to be, or describe oneself, as different from the gendered norm. This can make matters dizzying for the novice and pro alike, as there is no stable reference point for any identity given the sheer diversity of human language, culture, religion, and national context. Even the difference in feeling and narration from individual to individual can be overwhelming. But, helpfully, identity can't be isolated from the problems of everyday life, leading us toward how language, social institutions, and many bread-and-butter dimensions of the world are organized through a strict gender binary. Gender is not exclusively an identity. It is one of the most highly policed social categories that grants and limits access to the shared world. Instead of trying to memorize an ever-growing glossary of identities and terminologies, then, we can instead ask how gender organizes people's life possibilities. But where did the prevailing social segregation of gender come from? And why are Western cultures so anxious about defining and policing the boundaries of the binary gender system? In other words, why is the norm so restrictive if it doesn't seem to accommodate many people? The chapters in this part answer these questions by providing an important account of cultural change in the lived world.

Consider one common example of how the gender binary is made obligatory and administered in the United States today: identification documents. When a baby is born, its sex and gender are assigned on a birth certificate as required by state law. While we might reasonably expect that practice to be reliable if it is obligatory, many trans, nonbinary, and intersex people's lives are set up for difficulty by the arbitrariness and inaccuracy of the practice. A newborn can't tell a doctor, nurse, or parents anything about gender, so the cultural practice of Western medicine has been to make the determination based on genitals. In recent years, those genitals are generally observed during an ultrasound, months before birth. There isn't a deep scientific rationale behind the practice (there is no single scientific test that can definitively determine someone's sex or gender), so if that assignment proves to be incorrect over the course of a person's life, they will find it can be extremely difficult to change their birth certificate.

For decades trans people were generally unable to change their gender and sex markers at all or only through paying for expensive legal petitions on a case-by-case basis. Today there is a patchwork of different laws and regulations that vary by state, including anti-trans laws that explicitly try to prevent trans people from changing their birth certificates at all.[1] This causes major hardship. Many adults find that they are unable to change their gender marker on their driver's license, passport, and other government-issued ID because the state they were born in won't recognize the need to amend their birth certificate. This means that even if someone leaves a legally hostile state for another with more welcoming laws, they may never be able to escape the effects on their life of where they were born. And until recently many countries in Europe also required that trans people first be sterilized before changing their gender markers, a disturbing legacy of the eugenics movement.[2]

While it is certainly painful and alienating not to be described accurately on your birth certificate, the injury caused by binary government identification is less symbolic than material. Not appearing consistent with the gender marker on a driver's license, or in everyday paperwork, can result in widespread discrimination in public accommodation, employment, housing, and more. Trans people have been kicked off public transit, denied rental applications, and fired from their jobs for not looking like what their ID records them as— or for discrepancies across their papers.[3] Trans people are routinely subject to aggressive and sexualized searches in airport security because the invasive body scanning devices used by the Transportation Security Administration cannot reliably distinguish between different kinds of human bodies.[4] And disturbing practices of police brutality, sexual assault in jails and prisons, and housing of trans people with sex-segregated populations in psychiatric institutions, hospitals, and immigrant detention centers all reflect institutional cultures of abuse and violence.[5] If your ID makes you structurally out of place in a society organized by a rigid binary, your control over your body and your dignity can be taken away at a moment's notice. Trans activists and legal scholars call this situation *administrative violence*.[6] Much of the brutality of being excluded in law and policy is executed by bureaucratic and other state employees who have powerful discretion in affecting the quality of life of the trans people they encounter.

The ubiquity of gender surveillance and the bureaucratic weight of everyday life in the twenty-first century can make the discrimination or exclusion faced by trans people appear like an unintended consequence of a well-intentioned, if perhaps old-fashioned, way of organizing the world.[7] Yet as historians of racial segregation have shown, the construction of a separate and unequal world is hardly a natural outcome or an uncontested consensus. The world structured by a gender binary had to be built. From that point of view, the rational *fragility* of many binary systems is provocative. For instance, although Americans have been able to ask for an *X* on their passport instead of an *M* or *F* since 2021, there were *no* gender markers at all on US passports until 1977.[8] Louise Lawrence, a trans woman from the San Francisco Bay Area, succeeded in getting a passport under her name in 1958, only to have the State Department try after the fact to take it back.[9] There are many other examples worth considering.

Gender-segregated restrooms, for instance, were popularized in the nineteenth century. Moral crusaders aimed at the time to forcibly separate men and women along a public-private axis. This "separate spheres" ideology had deeply sexist intentions. Women were meant to be kept out of the public world, away from having any influence on politics or business. The women's bathroom was envisioned to be one place to confine women, who were seen as weak and in need of protection from the world by men.[10] Likewise, the gender segregation of sports was not based in a consensus that men and women couldn't compete for biological reasons. On the contrary, separate women's sports were most often created to keep women out of competition *because they were too competitive with men*.[11]

Each of these examples reveals in a different way that the cultural norm in Western countries of organizing the public world, law, and institutions through a gender binary has been highly contested. Indeed, cultural change *toward* a gender binary is yet another reminder that change is about the only constant when it comes to gender. Government IDs, bathrooms, and sports have not always been organized around a binary. And these examples suggest that the move away from a strict binary is a goal that many different groups marginalized by the binary might share, not just trans or nonbinary people. If gender is a shared category of subjection that affects everyone, then the transformation of cultural norms is a project that likewise involves everyone. Yet because trans and nonbinary people are especially targeted by a strict binary division of the world, their struggle to challenge norms has a lot to teach others.

The authors in part II delve into a range of high-profile challenges to norms that have made headlines in recent years, including pronouns, the segregation of bathrooms, the gendering of toys, coming out, and the Transgender Day of Visibility. Each of these case studies adds texture to the question of how we will decide to organize gender in everyday life in the future.

Notes

1. The Transgender Law Center maintains a "State-by-State Overview: Changing Gender Markers on Birth Certificates," https://transgender lawcenter.org/resources/id/state-by-state-overview-changing-gender -markers-on-birth-certificates.
2. Liam Stack, "European Court Strikes Down Required Sterilization for Transgender People," *New York Times*, April 12, 2017, https://www .nytimes.com/2017/04/12/world/europe/european-court-strikes-down -required-sterilization-for-transgender-people.html.
3. On the administrative and bureaucratic practices around identification, see Heath Fogg Davis, *Beyond Trans: Does Gender Matter?* (rpt., New York: New York University Press, 2018).
4. Allison Hope, "The Trauma of TSA for Trans Travelers," CNN, October 17, 2019, https://www.cnn.com/travel/article/tsa-body-scanners-transgender -travelers/index.html.

5. CeCe McDonald, *Captive Genders: Trans Embodiment and the Prison Industrial Complex*, 2nd ed., ed. Eric A. Stanley and Nat Smith (Oakland, CA: AK Press, 2015).

6. Dean Spade, *Normal Life: Administrative Violence, Critical Trans Politics, and the Limits of Law*, rev. and expanded ed. (Durham, NC: Duke University Press, 2015).

7. On the surveillance of gender and how it affects trans people, see Toby Beauchamp, *Going Stealth: Transgender Politics and U.S. Surveillance Practices*, illus. ed. (Durham, NC: Duke University Press, 2019).

8. Samantha Allen, "How the Rise of Androgyny Changed Our Passports," Daily Beast, October 14, 2018, https://www.thedailybeast.com/how-the-rise-of-androgyny-changed-our-passports; "U.S. Issues First Passport with 'X' Gender Marker," Reuters, October 27, 2021, https://www.reuters.com/world/us/us-issues-first-passport-with-x-gender-marker-2021-10-27/.

9. See Jules Gill-Peterson, "Toward a Historiography of the Lesbian Transsexual, or the TERF's Nightmare," *Journal of Lesbian Studies*, February 1, 2022, https://doi.org/10.1080/10894160.2021.1979726.

10. Jack D'Isidoro and T. J. Raphael, hosts, "The Sexist Origins of Gender-Segregated Bathrooms," *The Takeaway* (podcast), WNYC Studios, May 11, 2016, https://www.wnycstudios.org/podcasts/takeaway/segments/sexist-origins-gender-segregated-bathrooms.

11. Maya Wei-Haas and Jackie Mansky, "The Rise of the Modern Sportswoman," *Smithsonian Magazine*, August 18, 2016, https://www.smithsonianmag.com/science-nature/rise-modern-sportswoman-180960174/.

Chapter 6

What Are Gender Pronouns and Why Is It Important to Use the Right Ones?

GLEN HOSKING

GENDER PRONOUNS are the terms people choose to refer to themselves that reflect their gender identity. These might be he/him, she/her, or gender-neutral pronouns such as they/them. Knowing and using a person's chosen pronouns fosters inclusion, makes people feel respected and valued, and affirms their gender identity.[1]

The Difference between Sex and Gender

While people may use the terms *sex* and *gender* interchangeably, they mean different things.

Sex refers to the physical differences among people who are female, male, or intersex. A person typically has their sex assigned at birth based on physiological characteristics, including their genitalia and chromosome composition. This is distinct from gender, which is a social construct and reflects the social and cultural role of sex within a given community. People often develop their gender identity and gender expression in response to their environment.

While gender has been defined as binary in Western culture, gender in fact ranges along a spectrum; a person may identify at any point on this spectrum or outside it entirely. Gender is not neatly divided into the binary of "man" and "woman."[2] People may identify with a gender different from their sex assigned at birth; some people do not identify with any gender; still others identify with multiple genders. These identities may include transgender, nonbinary, or gender-neutral.

Only the person themself can determine what their gender identity is, and this can change over time.

Gender-Neutral Pronouns

People who identify outside the gender binary most often use nongendered or nonbinary pronouns that are not gender-specific. These include they/them/their used in the singular, ze (pronounced "zee") in place of she/he, and hir (pronounced "here") in place of his/him/her. Everyone has the right to use the gender pronouns that match their personal identity. These pronouns may or may not match their gender expression, such as how the person dresses, looks, behaves, or what name they go by.

Why the Right Pronouns Matter

It's important to support people's use of self-identified first names in place of legal names given at birth and their self-identified pronouns in place of assumed pronouns based on sex assigned at birth or others' perceptions of physical appearance. Being misgendered and/or misnamed may leave a person feeling disrespected, invalidated, and dismissed.[3] This can be distressing and threaten the person's mental health. Transgender and nonbinary people are twice as likely to have suicidal thoughts than the general population and are up to four times as likely to engage in risky substance use.[4]

Conversely, using correct pronouns and names reduces depression and suicide risks. Studies have found that young people who were able to use their chosen name and pronoun experienced 71 percent fewer symptoms of severe depression, a 34 percent decrease in reported thoughts of suicide, and a 65 percent decrease in suicide attempts when compared with peers who were not able to do so.[5]

7 Tips for Getting Pronouns Right

The following tips may help you better understand gender pronouns and how you can affirm someone's gender identity:

1. **Don't assume you know another person's gender or gender pronouns.**
   You can't always know what someone's gender pronouns are by looking at them, by their name, or by how they dress or behave.

2. **Ask a person what pronoun they use.**

   Asking about and correctly using someone's gender pronouns is an easy way to show your respect for their identity. Ask a person respectfully and privately what pronoun they use. A simple "Can I ask what pronoun you use?" will usually suffice.

3. **Share your own gender pronoun.**

   Normalize the sharing of gender pronouns by volunteering your own. You can include them after your name in your email signature, on your social media accounts, or when you introduce yourself in meetings. Normalizing the sharing of gender pronouns can be particularly helpful to people who use pronouns outside the binary.

4. **Apologize if you call someone by the wrong pronoun.**

   Mistakes happen, and it can be difficult to adjust to using someone's correct pronouns. If you accidentally misgender someone, apologize and continue the conversation using the correct pronoun.

5. **Avoid binary-gendered language.**

   Avoid addressing groups as "ladies and gentleman" or "boys and girls"; instead, address groups of people as "everyone," "colleagues," "friends," or "students." Employers should use gender-neutral language in formal and informal communications.

6. **Help others.**

   Help others use a person's correct pronouns. If a colleague, employer, or friend uses an incorrect pronoun, politely correct them.

7. Practice.

If you've not used gender-neutral pronouns such as *they* and *ze* before, give yourself time to practice and get used to them.

Notes

1. Elizabeth Smith, Tiffany Jones, Roz Ward, Jennifer Dixon, Anne Mitchell, and Lynne Hillier, *From Blues to Rainbows: The Mental Health and Well-Being of Gender Diverse and Transgender Young People in Australia* (Melbourne: Australian Research Centre in Sex, Health and Society, 2014), https://apo.org.au/node/41426.
2. Tim Newman, "Sex and Gender: Meanings, Definition, Identity, and Expression," *Medical News Today*, May 11, 2021, https://www.medicalnewstoday.com/articles/232363.
3. Smith et al., *From Blues to Rainbows.*
4. Christine S. Sinatra, "Victimization of Transgender Youths Linked to Suicidal Thoughts, Substance Abuse," College of Natural Sciences, University of Texas at Austin, September 18, 2017, https://cns.utexas.edu/news/victimization-of-transgender-youths-linked-to-suicidal-thoughts-substance-abuse.
5. Stephen T. Russell, Amanda M. Pollitt, Gu Li, and Arnold H. Grossman, "Chosen Name Use Is Linked to Reduced Depressive Symptoms, Suicidal Ideation, and Suicidal Behavior among Transgender Youth," *Journal of Adolescent Health* 63, no. 4 (2018): 503–5, https://doi.org/10.1016/j.jadohealth.2018.02.003.

Chapter 7

How Did Public Bathrooms Get to Be Separated by Sex in the First Place?

TERRY S. KOGAN

FOR YEARS, transgender rights activists have argued for their right to use the public restroom that aligns with their gender identity.

Some say that one solution to this impasse is to convert all public restrooms to unisex use, thereby eliminating the need even to consider a patron's sex. This might strike some as bizarre or drastic. Many assume that separating restrooms based on a person's biological sex is the "natural" way to determine who should and should not be permitted to use these public spaces.

In fact, however, laws in the United States did not address the issue of separating public restrooms by sex until the end of the 19th century, when Massachusetts became the first state to enact such a statute. By 1920, over 40 states had adopted similar legislation requiring that public restrooms be separated by sex.

So why did US states begin passing such laws? Were legislators merely recognizing natural anatomical differences between men and women?

I've studied the history of the legal and cultural norms that require the separation of public bathrooms by sex, and it's clear that there was nothing so benign about the enactment of these laws. Rather, these laws were rooted in the ideology of so-called separate spheres of the early 19th century: the idea that, in order to protect their virtue, women needed to stay at home to take care of children and household chores. In modern times, such a view of women's proper place would be readily dismissed as sexist. By highlighting the sexist origin of laws mandating sex separation of public restrooms, I hope to provide grounds for at least reconsidering their continued existence.

The Rise of a New American Ideology

During America's early history, the household was the center of economic production, the place where goods were made and sold.[1] That role of the home in the American economy changed at the end of the 18th century during the Industrial Revolution. As manufacturing became centralized in factories, men left for these new workplaces, while women remained in the home.

Soon, an ideological divide between public and private

spaces arose. The workplace and the public realm came to be considered the proper domain of men; the private realm of the home belonged to women. This divide lies at the heart of the separate spheres ideology.

The sentimental vision of the virtuous woman remaining on the homestead was a cultural myth that bore little resemblance to the evolving realities of the 19th century. From the century's outset, women emerged from the privacy of the home to enter the workplace and American civic life. For example, as early as 1822, when textile mills opened in Lowell, Massachusetts, young women began flocking to mill towns. Soon, single women constituted the overwhelming majority of the textile workforce. Women would also become involved in social reform and suffrage movements that required them to work outside the home.

Nonetheless, American culture didn't abandon the separate spheres ideology, and most moves by women outside the domestic sphere were viewed with suspicion and concern. By the middle of the 19th century, some scientists set their sights on reaffirming the ideology by undertaking research to prove that the female body was inherently weaker than the male body.[2]

Armed with such "scientific" facts (now understood as merely bolstering political views opposed to the emergent women's rights movement), legislators and other policy makers began enacting laws aimed at protecting "weaker" women

in the workplace. Examples included laws that limited women's work hours, laws that required a rest period for women during the workday or seats at their workstations, and laws that prohibited women from taking certain jobs and assignments considered dangerous.

Midcentury regulators also adopted architectural solutions to "protect" women who ventured outside the home. Architects and other planners began to cordon off various public spaces for the exclusive use of women. For example, a separate ladies' reading room—with furnishings that resembled those of a private home—became an accepted part of American public library design. In the 1840s, American railroads began designating a "ladies' car" for the exclusive use of women and their male escorts, and by the end of the 19th century, women-only parlor spaces had been created in other establishments, including photography studios, hotels, banks, and department stores.

Sex-Separated Restrooms: Putting Women in Their Place?

It was in this spirit that legislators enacted the first laws requiring that factory restrooms be separated by sex.

Well into the 1870s, toilet facilities in factories and other workplaces were overwhelmingly designed for one occupant and were often located outside buildings. These facilities emptied into unsanitary cesspools and privy vaults generally located beneath or adjacent to the factory. The possibility of indoor, multi-occupant restrooms didn't even arise until sanitation technology had developed to a stage where waste could be flushed into public sewer systems.

But by the late 19th century, the factory "water closet"—as restrooms were then called—became a flash point for a range of cultural anxieties. First, deadly cholera epidemics throughout the century had heightened concerns over public health. Soon, reformers known as "sanitarians" focused their attention on replacing the haphazard and unsanitary plumbing arrangements in homes and workplaces with technologically advanced public sewer systems.[3] Second, the rapid development of increasingly dangerous machinery in factories was viewed as a special threat to "weaker" female workers. Finally, Victorian values that stressed the importance of privacy and modesty were subjected to special challenge in factories, where women worked side by side with men, often sharing the same single-user restrooms.[4]

It was the confluence of these anxieties that led legislators in Massachusetts and other states to enact the first laws requiring that factory restrooms be sex-separated. Despite the ubiquity of women in the public realm, the spirit of the early-century separate spheres ideology was clearly reflected in this legislation. Understanding that "inherently weaker" women could not be forced back into the home, legislators opted instead to create a protective, homelike haven in the workplace for women by requiring separate restrooms, along with separate dressing rooms and resting rooms for women.

Thus, the historical justifications for the first laws in the United States requiring that public restrooms be separated by sex were not based on some notion that men's and women's restrooms were "separate but equal"—a gender-neutral policy that simply reflected anatomical differences. Rather, these laws were adopted as a way to further an early 19th-century moral ideology that dictated the appropriate role and place for women in society.

The Future of Public Restrooms

It is therefore surprising that this now-discredited notion has been resurrected in the current debate over who can use which public restrooms.

Opponents of transgender rights have employed the slogan "No Men in Women's Bathrooms," which evokes visions of weak women being subject to attack by men if transgender women are allowed to "invade" the public bathroom. In fact, the only solid evidence of any such attacks in public restrooms are those directed at transgendered individuals,[5] a significant percentage of whom report verbal or physical assault in such spaces. In the midst of the current maelstrom over public restrooms, it is important to keep in mind that our current laws mandating that public restrooms be separated by sex evolved from the separate spheres ideology of a bygone era.

Whether multi-occupancy unisex restrooms are the best solution or not, our lawmakers and the public need to begin envisioning new configurations of public restroom spaces, ones far more friendly to all people who move through public spaces.

Notes

1. Gary M. Walton and Hugh Rockoff, "The Economic Relations of the Colonies," chap. 4 in *History of the American Economy*, 11th ed. (Mason, OH: Cengage), 58–72.
2. Jerry Bergman, "Darwin's Teaching of Women's Inferiority," Institute for Creation Research, March 1, 1994, https://www.icr.org/article/darwins -teaching-womens-inferiority/.
3. Richard A. Pizzi, "Apostles of Cleanliness," *Modern Drug Discovery* 5, no. 5 (2022): 51–55, http://pubsapp.acs.org/subscribe/archive/mdd /v05/i05/html/05ttl.html?.
4. Nancy F. Cott, "Passionlessness: An Interpretation of Victorian Sexual Ideology, 1790–1850," *Signs: Journal of Women in Culture and Society* 4, no. 2 (1978): 219–36, https://doi.org/10.1086/493603.
5. Steve Wessler, "Vicious Beating of Woman Tragically Illustrates Restroom Safety Issues for Transgender People," *Steve Wessler* (blog), n.d., http://www.stevewessler.com/news/beating-of-woman-illustrates -restroom-safety-issues-for-transgender-people/.

Chapter 8

How Toys Became Gendered— and Why It'll Take More Than a Gender-Neutral Doll to Change How Boys Perceive Femininity

MEGAN K. MAAS

FIRST ANNOUNCED IN SEPTEMBER 2019, Mattel's line of gender-neutral dolls doesn't clearly signify as boy or girl. The dolls come with a variety of wardrobe options and can be outfitted with different lengths of hair. But can a doll—or the growing list of other gender-neutral toys—really change the way we think about gender?

Mattel says it's responding to research that shows "kids don't want their toys dictated by gender norms." One study found that 24 percent of US adolescents with a nontraditional sexual orientation or gender identity identified as bisexual or nonbinary,[1] so the decision makes business sense.

As a developmental psychologist who researches gender and sexual socialization, I can tell you that it also makes scientific sense. Gender is an identity and is not based on someone's biological sex. That's why I believe it's great news that some dolls will better reflect how children see themselves.

Unfortunately, a doll alone is not going to overturn decades of socialization that have led us to believe that boys wear blue, have short hair, and play with trucks, whereas girls wear pink, grow their hair long, and play with dolls. More to the point, it's not going to change how boys are taught that masculinity is good and femininity is something less—a view that my research shows is associated with sexual violence.

Pink Girls and Blue Boys

The kinds of toys American children play with tend to adhere to a clear gender binary. Toys marketed to boys are usual aggressive and involve action and excitement. Girl toys, on the other hand, are usually pink and passive, emphasizing beauty and nurturing.

It wasn't always like this.

Around the turn of the 20th century, toys were rarely marketed to different genders. By the 1940s, manufacturers quickly caught on to the idea that wealthier families would

buy an entire new set of clothing, toys, and other gadgets if the products were marketed differently for boys and girls. And so the idea of pink for girls and blue for boys was born.

Today, gendered toy marketing in the United States is stark. Walk down any toy aisle and you can clearly see who the audience is. The girl aisle is almost exclusively pink, showcasing mostly Barbie dolls and princesses. The boy aisle is mostly blue and features trucks and superheroes.

Breaking Down the Binary

The emergence of a gender-neutral doll is a sign of how this strict binary of boys' and girls' play is beginning to break down, at least when it comes to girls.

In a 2017 study, more than three-quarters of those surveyed said it was a good thing for parents to encourage young girls to play with toys or do activities "associated with the opposite gender," whereas more than 80 percent of women and millennials said it was a good thing.[2] But when it came to boys, support for gender-divergent play dropped significantly, with 64 percent overall—and far fewer men— saying it was good to encourage boys to do things associated with girls. Those who were older or more conservative were even more likely to think it wasn't a good idea.

Reading between the lines suggests there's a view that traits stereotypically associated with men—such as strength, courage, and leadership—are good, whereas those tied to femininity—such as vulnerability, emotion, and caring—are bad. Thus boys receive the message that wanting to look up to girls is not OK. And many boys are taught over and over throughout their lives that exhibiting "female traits" is wrong and means they aren't "real men." Worse, they're frequently punished for it,[3] while exhibiting masculine traits like aggression is often rewarded.

How This Affects Sexual Expectations

This gender socialization continues into adulthood and affects our romantic and sexual expectations.

For example, a 2015 study I conducted with three coauthors explored how participants thought their gender affected their sexual experiences. Roughly 45 percent of women said they expected to experience some kind of sexual violence just because they are women; conversely, none of the men reported a fear of sexual violence, and 35 percent said their manhood meant they should expect pleasure.[4]

These findings can be linked back to the kinds of toys we play with.

Girls are taught to be passive and strive for beauty by playing with princesses and putting on makeup. Boys are encouraged to be more active or even aggressive with trucks, toy guns, and action figures; building, fighting, and even dominating are emphasized. An analysis of Lego sets demonstrated this dichotomy in what they emphasized—for boys: building expertise and skilled professions; for girls: caring for others, socializing, and being pretty.[5] Thus, girls spend their childhood practicing how to be pretty and to care for another person, while boys practice getting what they want.

This results in a sexual double standard in which men are the powerful actors and women are subordinate objects. Even in cases of sexual assault, research has shown that people will put more blame on a female rape victim if she does something that violates a traditional gender role, such as cheating on her husband, which is more accepted for men than for women.[6] A 2016 study found that adolescent men who subscribed to traditional masculine gender norms were more likely to engage in dating violence, such as sexual assault, physical or emotional abuse, and stalking.[7]

Teaching Gender Appreciation

Mattel's Creatable World gender-neutral dolls offer much-needed variety in kids' toys, but children, as well as adults, also need to learn to have more tolerance for others who express gender differently from how they do. And boys in particular need support in appreciating and practicing more traditional feminine traits, like communicating emotion or caring for someone else—skills that are required for any healthy relationship.

Gender neutrality represents the absence of gender, not

the appreciation of different gender expression. If we empha-
size only the former, I believe femininity and the people who
express it will remain devalued.

So, consider doing something gender-nonconforming
with your children's existing dolls, such as having Barbie win a
wrestling championship or giving Ken a tutu. And encourage
the boys in your life to play with them too.

Notes

1. Ryan J. Watson, Christopher W. Wheldon, and Rebecca M. Puhl, "Ev-
    idence of Diverse Identities in a Large National Sample of Sexual and
    Gender Minority Adolescents," Journal of Research on Adolescence 30,
    no. S2 (2019): 431–42, https://doi.org/10.1111/jora.12488.
2. Juliana Menasce Horowitz, "Most Americans See Value in Steering
    Children toward Toys, Activities Associated with Opposite Gender,"
    Pew Research Center, December 19, 2017, https://www.pewresearch
    .org/fact-tank/2017/12/19/most-americans-see-value-in-steering
    -children-toward-toys-activities-associated-with-opposite-gender/.
3. Ashleigh Shelby Rosette, Jennifer S. Mueller, and R. David Lebel, "Are
    Male Leaders Penalized for Seeking Help? The Influence of Gender and
    Asking Behaviors on Competence Perceptions," Leadership Quarterly 26,
    no. 5 (2015), 749–62, https://doi.org/10.1016/j.leaqua.2015.02.001.
4. Megan K. Maas, Cindy L. Shearer, Meghan M. Gillen, and Eva S. Lefkowitz.
    "Sex Rules: Emerging Adults' Perceptions of Gender's Impact on Sexuali-
    ty," Sexuality & Culture 19, no. 4 (2015): 617–36. https://doi.org/10.1007
    /s12119-015-9281-6.
5. Stephanie M. Reich, Rebecca W. Black, and Tammie Foliaki, "Constructing
    Difference: LEGO® Set Narratives Promote Stereotypic Gender Roles and
    Play," Sex Roles 79, nos. 5–6 (2018): 285–98, https://doi.org/10.1007
    /s11199-017-0868-2.
6. G. Tendayi Viki and Dominic Abrams, "But She Was Unfaithful: Benevolent
    Sexism and Reactions to Rape Victims Who Violate Traditional Gender
    Role Expectations," Sex Roles 47, nos. 5–6 (2002): 289–93, https://doi
    .org/10.1023/a:1021342912248.
7. H. Luz McNaughton Reyes, Vangie A. Foshee, Phyllis Holditch Niolon,
    Dennis E. Reidy, and Jeffrey E. Hall, "Gender Role Attitudes and Male
    Adolescent Dating Violence Perpetration: Normative Beliefs as Mod-
    erators," Journal of Youth and Adolescence 45, no. 2 (2016): 350–60,
    https://doi.org/10.1007/s10964-015-0278-0.

Chapter 9

Trans Youth Are Coming Out and Living in Their Gender Much Earlier than Older Generations

JAE A. PUCKETT

THERE ARE A FEW common identity milestones that transgender, or trans, people experience across their lives.[1] One
of the milestones is starting to feel different from the sex
assigned to them at birth. Another is identifying with a trans
identity—for instance, as a trans man or genderqueer person,
meaning they don't identify with a binary gender such as a
woman or a man. There also is the experience of living in line
with this identity, which can include disclosing it to others and
making changes to one's name, pronouns, and appearance.

And then there's accessing gender-affirming medical care such as puberty blockers, hormones, or surgeries.

These milestones can happen at any age in a person's life, despite the stereotype that trans people must have always known they were trans. Some people may not pass all the milestones. And although these are common milestones, they are not exhaustive, and no singular narrative captures all trans people's experiences.

As an assistant professor of psychology at Michigan State University and the director of Trans-ilience, a community-engaged research team, I study how stigma and oppression influence mental health, as well as ways of being resilient in the face of such challenges. Recognizing that there is no one way to be trans, I surveyed 695 trans individuals aged 16 to 70 years.[2] My collaborators, Samantha Tornello, Brian Mustanski, and Michael Newcomb, and I explored how common identity milestones for transgender people may relate to mental health and how generations experience these milestones differently. Our peer-reviewed study was published in early 2021.[3]

Baby Boomers to Gen Z

Our research showed that Generation Z, born between 1997 and 2012, and millennials, born between 1981 and 1996, are more diverse in their gender identities than older generations.

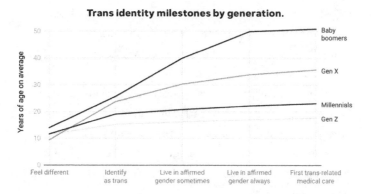

Trans identity milestones by generation.

Years of age on average

50 · Baby boomers
40 · Gen X
30 · Millennials
20 · Gen Z
10 ·
0

Feel different | Identify as trans | Live in affirmed gender sometimes | Live in affirmed gender always | First trans-related medical care

This is particularly true when it comes to identifying as gender-queer, nonbinary, and agender. For example, 24.5 percent of Gen Z participants identified as nonbinary, whereas only 7.4 percent of baby boomers identified this way.

The Generation X participants, born between 1965 and 1980, and baby boomers, born between 1946 and 1964, were more likely to identify as trans women compared with younger participants. And overall, trans women reported later ages when starting to live in their affirmed gender and receiving gender-affirming medical care, relative to the other gender groups. Trans women were, on average, around 31 years old when living in their affirmed gender all of the time; other gender groups ranged from 21 to 25 years old.

We found little difference between the generations for when they recognized that their gender felt different from their sex assigned at birth. On average, this happened around age 11, with the youngest age reported for this milestone being 2 years old.

However, the boomers reported reaching the other major

milestones later than younger groups. For example, boomers were, on average, around age 50 when they were living in their affirmed gender all the time. In contrast, Gen X was 34, millennials were 22, and Gen Z was 17.

Gen Z and millennials also reported much shorter gaps between reaching milestones. For instance, boomers reported an average 24-year delay between starting to identify as trans and living in their affirmed gender. There were just a two-year gap and a three-year gap for Gen Z and millennials, respectively.

Notably, there can be many challenges to coming out and living in an affirmed gender that should also be taken into account. These barriers include living with a family that is not supportive, being concerned about violent attacks, and not having access to appropriate medical care.

Mental Health Advantages

When trans people affirm their gender, our study found there to be clear benefits to their mental health. Regardless of the age at which they experienced milestones, respondents who reported living in an affirmed gender and accessing trans-related medical care reported less internalized stigma, anxiety and depression, and what researchers call gender nonaffirmation, such as being misgendered, which includes others using the wrong pronouns for the individual or disrespecting their gender. Reaching these milestones is also associated with higher levels of appearance congruence, meaning that a person's appearance represents their gender identity. This, too, is associated with lower levels of depression and anxiety.

Given these findings, supporting trans people in affirming their gender identity can benefit their mental health and well-being. Support can mean addressing family, school, and legal realms so that trans people are respected and supported.

Despite the benefits of affirming one's gender, the younger generations reported greater stressors—such as internalized stigma or invalidation of their gender—and symptoms of depression and anxiety compared with older generations. In other words, it appears that younger trans people are facing greater mental health challenges and exposure to stressors, even while they are coming out and affirming their gender at a younger age. It may be that as trans people age, they develop resilience and resistance strategies that help them navigate oppression while improving their health and well-being.

Ongoing Violence and Discrimination

It's difficult for trans people to come out and affirm their gender identity in a society where they—especially trans people of color—are targets of violence and murder,[4] their histories are erased, and their rights are under attack. In light of my team's findings, supporting and validating trans people is a meaningful way to reduce the health disparities in this marginalized community.[5]

Notes

1. Lindsey Wilkinson, Jennifer Pearson, and Hui Liu, "Educational Attainment of Transgender Adults: Does the Timing of Transgender Identity Milestones Matter?," *Social Science Research* 74 (2018): 146–60, https://doi.org/10.1016/j.ssresearch.2018.04.006.
2. Kevin L. Nadal, Avy Skolnik, and Yinglee Wong, "Interpersonal and Systemic Microaggressions toward Transgender People: Implications for Counseling," *Journal of LGBT Issues in Counseling* 6, no. 1 (2012): 55–82, https://doi.org/10.1080/15538605.2012.648583.
3. Jae A. Puckett, Samantha Tornello, Brian Mustanski, and Michael E. Newcomb, "Gender Variations, Generational Effects, and Mental Health of

Transgender People in Relation to Timing and Status of Gender Identity Milestones," *Psychology of Sexual Orientation and Gender Diversity* (2021): https://doi.org/10.1037/sgd0000391.

4. Rebecca L. Stotzer, "Violence against Transgender People: A Review of United States Data," *Aggression and Violent Behavior* 14, no. 3 (2009): 170–79, https://doi.org/10.1016/j.avb.2009.01.006.

5. Lily Durwood, Katie A. McLaughlin, and Kristina R. Olson. "Mental Health and Self-Worth in Socially Transitioned Transgender Youth," *Journal of the American Academy of Child & Adolescent Psychiatry* 56, no. 2 (2017): 116–23, https://doi.org/10.1016/j.jaac.2016.10.016.

Chapter 10

Trans Day of Visibility
Offers Chance for Community to
Stand in Solidarity and Support

JAY A. IRWIN

VISIBILITY WITHIN the transgender community is often a catch-22, especially for trans people of color or those living in rural, conservative areas. Hiding one's identity can be a damaging experience and can increase feelings of isolation, stigma, and shame.[1] But standing out as a trans person can make someone a target for discrimination or violence.[2] As a trans man who studies transgender health and well-being, I believe Trans Day of Visibility—celebrated annually on March 31—is an important day for community members to come together and find support and solidarity in knowing they are not alone.

A Celebration's History

Trans Day of Visibility acknowledges the contributions made by people within the transgender, nonbinary, and gender-diverse communities (hereafter referred to as "trans," to encompass anyone who doesn't identify with their sex assigned at birth). Rachel Crandall, a transgender activist from Michigan, organized the first Trans Day of Visibility in 2009. By 2014, the day was being celebrated internationally.

Before then, the only day of recognition the trans community had was Transgender Day of Remembrance, a day of mourning held on November 20 to commemorate trans people who died in the previous year. Trans Day of Visibility, then, is an attempt, as the trans community puts it, to "give us our roses while we're still here."

In 2015, I and other local trans activists in Omaha, Nebraska, hosted the first of several annual events for our community. It featured panels, question-and-answer sessions, and support groups for family members, trans people themselves, and cisgender, or cis, people—which refers to people who identify with the sex they were assigned at birth—who wanted to learn how to be better allies to the trans community. Some of us wore T-shirts that said, "Ask Me I'm Trans," on the day of the event to facilitate dialogue between the trans and cis communities.

Fighting Stigma

Visibility as a transgender person is not a one-size-fits-all approach for people within the trans community. Some people may embrace visibility, while others, for comfort, safety, or other deeply personal reasons, may not feel comfortable being visibly trans.

After all, threats of violence within the trans community are not uniformly distributed. Trans women of color are most at risk,[3] as they often face multiple forms of discrimination,[4] including transphobia, racism, classism, misogyny, and misogynoir[5]— the unique misogyny that Black women face. Because of job discrimination, roughly 20 percent of trans people engage in the underground economy, including commercial sex work, and may confront additional transphobic discrimination as a result of their work.

Trans Day of Visibility is an attempt to break these cycles of violence and discrimination against trans people.

Ongoing Challenges

At times during the COVID-19 pandemic, trans people were largely unable to provide in-person support to one another, and those who underwent physical changes couldn't fully celebrate those changes with friends.

Furthermore, we have seen an escalation in legislation that targets trans people with sports bans and attempts to limit their access to health care. Over 20 states introduced at least one anti-trans bill in 2020. That kind of coordinated policy campaign against a very small community—estimated to be less than 1 percent of the US population—sends a pointed message to the trans community that we are not welcome.

It's a message that I believe could be counterbalanced if we could gather in support of one another. I can attest that there's something powerful about being in a room full of trans people. The love, support, and understanding are unlike anything else I've experienced.

Trans Day of Visibility focuses on trans people but is not exclusive to the trans community. Allies of the trans community can also take part by reaching out to a trans friend and lending their support. Those who live in a state that is trying to enact anti-trans legislation can write to their state legislator to oppose the bill. Within their social circles, allies can be visible and vocal supporters of trans people.

Notes

1. Walter O. Bockting, Michael H. Miner, Rebecca E. Swinburne Romine, Autumn Hamilton, and Eli Coleman, "Stigma, Mental Health, and Resilience in an Online Sample of the US Transgender Population," *American Journal of Public Health* 103, no. 5 (2013): 943–51, https://doi.org/10.2105/ajph.2013.301241.

2. Lisa R. Miller and Eric Anthony Grollman, "The Social Costs of Gender Non-conformity for Transgender Adults: Implications for Discrimination and Health," *Sociological Forum* 30, no. 3 (2015): 809–31, https://doi.org/10.1111/socf.12193.

3. Laurel Westbrook, *Unlivable Lives: Violence and Identity in Transgender Activism* (Berkeley: University of California Press, 2020).

4. Salvador Vidal-Ortiz, "The Figure of the Transwoman of Color through the Lens of 'Doing Gender,'" *Gender & Society* 23, no. 1 (2009): 99–103, https://doi.org/10.1177/0891243208326461.

5. Elías Cosenza Krell, "Is Transmisogyny Killing Trans Women of Color? Black Trans Feminisms and the Exigencies of White Femininity," *TSQ: Transgender Studies Quarterly* 4, no. 2 (2017): 226–42, https://doi.org/10.1215/23289252-3815033.

Chapter 11

Transgender People of Color Face Unique Challenges as Gender Discrimination and Racism Intersect

GABRIEL M. LOCKETT, JULES SOSTRE,
and **ROBERTO L. ABREU**

THROUGHOUT HISTORY, transgender people of color have had a place of honor in many Indigenous cultures around the world. This changed in many places, however, when European colonizers began forcing Indigenous people to follow white social norms. These include anti–Blackness, Christianity, and a gender binary that reduced gender to just man or woman. Colonizers presumed that being cisgender, or having a gender identity that is congruent with gender assigned at birth, was the only acceptable norm.

For trans people who refused or were unable to conform, colonial societies often used racism and cis-sexism, or behaviors and beliefs that assume the inferiority of trans people, to invalidate their existence, limit their access to resources, and threaten their well-being. For example, colonizers in some cases deemed people who expressed their gender outside the binary as sinful and deviant, and punished them with emotional and physical violence.[1]

The reverberations of these colonial beliefs are still felt today. In just the first three months of 2022, there were over 154 anti-trans state bills proposed across the United States seeking to limit the rights of trans kids and their parents. And for trans people of color, the challenges they face because of gender discrimination are exacerbated by struggles they deal with because of racism.

We are researchers who study how LGBTQ people of color build resilience, resist oppression, and promote wellness within their communities. We look at how having multiple identities like being trans and a person of color intersect and interact with each other in ways that affect how someone navigates their life. Trans people of color who have multiple marginalized identities face higher levels of stress from being a minority compared with those with fewer marginalized identities.[2] While there has been a lack of research on the experiences of trans people of color,[3] studies suggest that many of the challenges they face arise from the intersection of racism, xenophobia, and cisnormativity.

Common Challenges and Barriers

The health care system has historically been fraught with danger for trans people of color. Over the years, people of color have been experimented on without consent, denied ownership over their own test results and bodies, and barred access to care. Some have played critical roles in transforming medical research and science without any knowledge of doing so. Mistrust gets magnified for trans people of color when they are deadnamed (called by the birth name they no longer go by), misgendered, or racially discriminated against—all of which may happen in one medical appointment.

Medical professionals and lawmakers have also mandated gatekeeping measures that require extra steps to qualify for gender-affirming care such as hormones and surgery. Trans people are asked to prove that they have a persistent experience of gender dysphoria, defined as an incongruence between one's gender assigned at birth and one's gender identity. Such insistence treats being transgender as an illness to be cured based on what cisgender people believe bodies should look like. It erases gender euphoria, or a feeling of joy or satisfaction associated with a gender different from what one was assigned at birth, as a reason for pursuing transition.

With only a limited number of providers who can competently and respectfully help them navigate these life-changing services, trans people of color are often left to fend for themselves. With legislation on the books that outlaws gender-affirming treatment for trans kids, they and their families are forced to travel long distances to obtain care or not have access to care at all.

Continuous exposure to stressors resulting from this discrimination has negative physical and mental health consequences for trans people of color. And these challenges are compounded by other common stressors, including homelessness, employment discrimination, and restricted access to legal documentation, among others.

Targets of Violence

Trans people of color face disproportionate rates of violence as a result of racism and transphobia. Compared with their cis peers, trans people are four times more likely to be a victim of a violent crime.

And trans people of color have been the overwhelming targets of this violence. The Human Rights Campaign recorded over 256 cases of fatal violence against trans people from 2013 to 2021 in the United States, 84 percent of whom were people of color. In 2021 alone, 57 trans people were killed, and more than half were Black trans women. Black trans women continue to have the highest risk for violence owing to how their experiences of anti-Black racism, cis-sexism, and sexism intersect (also known as transmisogynoir). The true numbers are likely to be much higher. Many hate crimes go unreported, due to both fear that one's identity will be questioned and a lack of trust in law enforcement.

Additionally, trans people of color often experience violence from police and other law enforcement officials. A 2015 report by the National Center for Transgender Equality in the United States found that 58 percent of trans people reported being harassed, abused, or mistreated during their interactions with police. It also noted that police frequently assumed that trans women of color were sex workers.[4] A 2021 study showed that trans Latinx immigrants and asylum seekers who entered the United States often experienced torture and were denied basic medical care in detention facilities.[5]

Resilience and Strength

Trans people of color have found multiple strategies to help them navigate and overcome these challenges.

One is to build resilience by coping with and adapting to stressors and adversities. Many trans people of color draw strength from supportive role models and members of their community. Being a positive role model themselves and having a strong sense of their own self-worth are also key factors to building resilience.

For example, one trans person of color who survived a traumatic event shared with researchers that resilience for them meant having pride in their gender and racial and ethnic identity, while also recognizing and negotiating the challenges they face because of systemic oppression. They also built resilience by engaging in activism, advocating for themselves, and connecting with trans communities of color.[6]

Trans people of color continue to find strength in collective action. Trans women of color have been at the forefront of social justice movements, and Black trans women have been a central driving force in the fight for LGBTQ rights.

Toward Liberation

There are countless ways to support trans people of color working toward liberation.

One way is self-education. This includes learning about privilege and how it gives select groups power over others in ways that range from microaggressions to physical violence. It is important to note that self-education is a continuous process that requires humility.

Another way is to keep up with attacks against marginalized communities and to be a co-conspirator in resisting such attacks. Instead of just being a passive ally, ask how you can leverage your privilege to support trans people of color. This could be working to provide inclusive and safe work environments, schools, and medical systems. It could also take the form of equitably compensating trans people of color for their labor.

Finally, call in and call out.[7] That is, speak up when someone is harming a trans person of color; or, if you're the one who's called out, then listen and take responsibility.

Notes

1. Jeremy D. Kidd and Tarynn M. Witten, "Transgender and Transsexual Identities: The Next Strange Fruit—Hate Crimes, Violence and Genocide against the Global Trans-Communities," *Journal of Hate Studies* 6, no. 1 (2007), 31–64, https://doi.org/10.33972/jhs.47.

2. Kali Cyrus, "Multiple Minorities as Multiply Marginalized: Applying the Minority Stress Theory to LGBTQ People of Color," *Journal of Gay & Lesbian Mental Health* 21, no. 3 (2017): 194–202, https://doi.org/10.1080 /19359705.2017.1320739.

3. Andrew P. Barnett, Ana María del Río-González, Benjamin Parchem, Veronica Pinho, Rodrigo Aguayo-Romero, Nadine Nakamura, Sarah K. Calabrese, Paul J. Poppen, and Maria Cecilia Zea, "Content Analysis of Psychological Research with Lesbian, Gay, Bisexual, and Transgender People of Color in the United States: 1969–2018" *American Psychologist* 74, no. 8 (2019): 898–911, https://doi.org/10.1037/amp0000562.

4. Sandy E. James, Jody L. Herman, Susan Rankin, Mara Keisling, Lisa Mottet, and Ma'ayan Anaf, *The Report of the 2015 U.S. Transgender Survey* (Washington, DC: National Center for Transgender Equality, 2016), https://transequality.org/sites/default/files/docs/usts/USTS-Full-Report -Dec17.pdf. The next U.S. Trans Survey is taking place in 2022.

5. Laura P. Minero, Sergio Domínguez Jr., Stephanie L. Budge, and Bamby Salcedo, "Latinx Trans Immigrants' Survival of Torture in US Detention: A Qualitative Investigation of the Psychological Impact of Abuse and Mistreatment," *International Journal of Transgender Health* 23, nos. 1–2 (2022): 36–59, https://www.tandfonline.com/doi/full/10.1080/26895269 .2021.1938779.

6. RESULTS, *Responding to Oppressive Behavior at RESULTS: Resource Guide*, n.d., https://results.org/wp-content/uploads/Call-in_Call-Out _Resource_Guide.pdf.

7. RESULTS, *Responding to Oppressive Behavior.*

Part III

Transgender Youth and Children

Transgender children seem to have burst onto the world stage in recent years. For better or for worse, gender diversity is increasingly associated with youth itself. Does this mean there are more trans and nonbinary young people today than in past generations? Are today's youth profoundly shifting how gender is imagined and represented? How are trans children surviving the incredible danger and backlash of being made into the generational symbols of gender diversity? And what role do parents and other adults play in supporting trans youth? What do we need to learn to care for and support children?

The sheer scale of the conversation around trans young people today is overwhelming in many ways, and the chatter often drowns out the voices of the kids themselves. A range of adult pundits, politicians, and medical skeptics have claimed that today's youth have had *too much* access to transition. While that is easy to disprove as a matter of fact, these commentators often mean to suggest more seriously that, at the very least, trans youth should be made to wait longer to transition, as if waiting were not a cruel and painful experience. These concerned adults often provide the justification that we don't yet understand, or young people themselves can't understand, what it means to transition. Isn't trans childhood a new proposition?

If we listen to trans young people, we might find that our adult anxieties are the actual problem. Here is what an 18-year-old trans girl wrote to the doctor Harry Benjamin in 1965, after he told her to wait a few years before accessing medical transition (the medical age of consent at the time was 21): "You see I've wanted to have an operation like this for several years, and now is as good a time as any. I don't want to wait until I'm growing old. I want to be a girl on the way to my old age. I want to be a girl now so that I can grow up the rest of the way as a normal girl."[1] There is a simplicity born of confidence in this girl's letter. She already knew what she needed, and she wanted to live as a girl during her youth because growing up as a girl was what any non–trans girl would be entitled to. Far from an unprecedented ethical dilemma or experimental medical question of the present, trans young people have seemingly been having the same conversation with adults for over 50 years at this point.

In fact, the evidence stretches back even farther. In *Histories of the Transgender Child*, I wrote about a trans woman I call Val, who was working tirelessly in the late 1940s to get access to gender-affirmation surgery in Wisconsin. While waiting on the doctors squabbling over whether to grant her request, she gave a life history to a psychologist in which she spoke about her childhood decades earlier. At the beginning of the 1930s, Val had been accepted as a girl by her family without any medical diagnosis required. When the time came for her to start school, her parents had spoken with the administration, as well as the local judge in their rural town, to make sure she could attend as a girl. Val was able to use the girl's restroom and join the 4-H club like her fellow girl classmates. Everyone in her life at that time respected her and treated her as a girl. Her identity wasn't seen as a problem or a crisis. Val is one of the remarkable trans children from over 90 years ago who make it impossible to claim that trans youth are new or unprecedented. Yet even the fact that Val had already lived an adult trans life for years by the late 1940s did not guarantee that her wait would end. Val's request for surgery in the Wisconsin hospital was denied.[2]

If adults have been telling trans children to wait for nearly a century, what exactly will it take to admit that there is no ethical basis to stop kids from being trans? In some ways trans youth today face a worse situation than those whom I write about in *Histories of the Transgender Child*. Today, trans children and youth must learn to survive in a world in which everyone has been taught to look for them, identify them, and bully them. As difficult as Val's childhood might have been in the absence of widely known trans language to describe her, her attending school as a girl and using the girls' restroom didn't lead Wisconsin to pass laws trying to stop her from participating in everyday life. Nowadays the subject of trans children and youth is, unlike in the 1930s, highly dramatized and politicized. As I explain in the preface to this book, trans young people are the targets of a global network of political violence. In that campaign against trans children's wishes and dignity, there is powerful and ubiquitous disinformation circulating about trans childhood not just on social media but also in newspapers of record and in congressional testimony.[3] This ecosystem of disinformation, much of which centers around distortions or outright fictions about gender-affirming medicine for young people, is designed to fan the flames of adult anxiety and hatred.

The authors in part III of this book are deeply aware of how badly high-quality research is needed in a knowledge economy as deliberately distorted as this one. The authors therefore prioritize clear and reliable information that they and their colleagues have dedicated their careers to pursuing through research and practice. Importantly, the contributions are geared toward the genre of advice for anxious and confused adults, as it is so often us adults who are creating the problems we project onto children. Parents, caregivers, educators, and the public all deserve access to properly researched, vetted, and useful information. The contributors, many of whom work directly with trans young people, are prepared to answer a series of pressing questions: What does the clinical model of gender identity development say about childhood? What work do parents and guardians need to do to be present and supportive of children who have come out to them? How do adults become champions of youth and deal with hostile environments at school or college? And how can we build a less rigidly gendered world for children to let all of them thrive?

The stakes in answering these questions are very high, as failing to support trans children and young people comes with the cost of lives lost or diminished through unnecessary suffering. But perhaps equally important, the multidisciplinary research assembled in this part is portable. By sharing this information with caring, loving adults who support young people, we can begin collectively to *de-dramatize* trans childhood. Part of the danger that trans children and youth face is that their lives are treated as emergencies from all sides, making it impossible for them to breathe. The pressure on young people today is staggering. Anti-trans forces targeting young people treat transition or even changing pronouns and clothes as the dramatic end of Western society. But even the defenders and allies of trans youth can reinforce the idea that to be a trans child is, in some way, a tragedy. Even if we understand the pain and suffering of young people to be a terrible failing in our duty to care for them by respecting their humanity, it is harmful in and of itself to tie trans childhood over and over to the most damaging tropes, including the specter of depression and suicide. This is not to minimize their impact but rather to understand that trans children's lives deserve to be seen as valuable on their own terms, too.

When we begin to reject the dramatic narrative that treats trans children as tragic and undesirable, as if no one could ever wish that a child be trans, we can start tending to the deep wounds we have inflicted on these remarkable young people. When we learn to see trans people as one of many benign variations in human biology and culture, we can learn to wish that there be trans children in the world. We can learn to greet trans childhood not as a sad or regretful sentence that some children must endure but instead as a happy event in the world. We must learn to want there to be trans children in the world if we are going to end the formidable and routinized harm we adults inflict on them every single day.

The chapters in part III remind us that, as we adults learn to listen and value the gift of sharing the world with trans and nonbinary youth, we are called to act on the alarming set of vulnerabilities trans and nonbinary kids face because of how they are treated in a culture that does not value their self-knowledge and dreams. There is nothing wrong with trans children or in living a trans childhood. But there is something deeply unjust about a world that would punish them for existing—and for having the courage to tell us who they are.

Notes

1. J. A. to Harry Benjamin, January 1965, Harry Benjamin Collection, box 3, Library and Special Collections, Kinsey Institute for Research in Sex, Gender and Reproduction, Indiana University, Bloomington, Indiana.
2. Jules Gill-Peterson, *Histories of the Transgender Child* (Minneapolis: University of Minnesota Press, 2018), 61–64.
3. For longer treatments of this disinformation campaign and its relationship to anti-trans political movements, see Jules Gill-Peterson, "The Anti-trans Lobby's Real Agenda," *Jewish Currents*, April 27, 2021, https://jewishcurrents.org/the-anti-trans-lobbys-real-agenda; and Jules Gill-Peterson, "From Gender Critical to QAnon: Anti-trans Politics and the Laundering of Conspiracy," *New Inquiry*, September 13, 2021, https://thenewinquiry.com/from-gender-critical-to-qanon-anti-trans-politics-and-the-laundering-of-conspiracy/.

Chapter 12

When Do Children Develop Their Gender Identity?

VANESSA LOBUE

GENDER IS GENERALLY thought of as a stable trait: we are born male or female, and we stay that way as we grow from small children to adults. It turns out, though, that for young children, initial concepts about gender are quite flexible.

In my own research, I've found that children don't begin to notice and adopt gender-stereotyped behaviors (e.g., preferring colors like pink or blue) until the age of two or three years. A few years later, their concept of gender becomes quite rigid, and although it becomes more relaxed by middle childhood, even adults have trouble going back to thinking about gender as something that's flexible.

So, how do children come to understand gender? When do they begin to think about gender as a stable trait?

What Is Gender?

We often tend to think about gender as the biological differences between men and women. It is true that the path to gender development begins at conception. Each cell in our body has 46 chromosomes. A father's sperm and a mother's egg each has only half: 23 each. At conception, the chromosomes of the sperm and the egg match up into 22 identical pairs, with pair 23 being the sex chromosome. In most cases, XX chromosomes will become female and XY chromosomes will become male.

But this isn't always the case. Gender is what actually gets expressed—how we look, how we act, and how we feel. While sex is determined by what is written into the chromosomes or what is dictated by our biology, known as genotype, it is the interaction between the genes (genotype) and the environment that determines gender. The biological sex of babies may not determine their gender later. Sex doesn't necessarily map onto gender perfectly, and the environment plays a role in determining the gender of each person.[1]

Perhaps this shouldn't be that surprising, given that sex in many species of animals is determined entirely by environmental circumstances and not by their biology. For example, there are animals that don't have sex chromosomes at all, and some species of coral reef fish can actually switch genders if their school requires it. Alligators, crocodiles, turtles, and some lizards don't have sex chromosomes either; their sex is determined by the temperature of their nest during incubation.

It's true that most of the time, a person's sex and gender are quite similar, but this doesn't have to be the case. And of late, the lines between sex and gender are becoming more blurred as people are becoming more comfortable identifying as transgender, or with a gender that is not consistent with their sex. In fact, for some people, gender is nonbinary; it exists instead on a spectrum of masculinity and femininity.

Children's Early Gender Concepts

So it turns out that gender is a more flexible state than most people think. And we start out as children thinking more flexibly about gender than we end up. Before the age of five, children don't seem to think that gender has any permanence at all. A preschooler might ask his female teacher whether she was a boy or girl when she was little, or a young boy might say that he wants to grow up to be a mommy. Research supports this early flexibility in children's gender concepts.

For example, in a well-known study, psychologist Sandra Bem showed preschool-aged children three photographs of a male and a female toddler.[2] In the first photo, the toddler was naked; in the second one, the toddler was dressed in gender-typical clothing (e.g., a dress and pigtails for the girl, a collared shirt for the boy holding a football); in the third photo, the toddler was dressed in stereotypical clothing of the opposite gender. Bem then asked the children a variety of questions. First, she asked them about the photo of the naked toddler and the photo of the toddler dressed in gender-typical clothing, inquiring whether the toddler was a boy or a girl. She then presented the children with the same toddler dressed in opposite-gendered clothing. She told them that the toddler was playing a silly dress-up game and made sure that the first nude photo of the toddler was still visible for reference. She then asked the children whether the toddler in the third photograph was still a boy or a girl.

Most three- to five-year-olds thought that a boy who decided to dress up like a girl was now indeed a girl. It wasn't until children understood that boys have penises and girls have vaginas that they also knew that changing your clothes doesn't change your gender.

Developing Gender Identity

Further research suggests that children's concept of gender develops gradually between the ages of three and five.[3] After the age of five, most children believe that outward changes in clothing or hairstyle don't constitute a change in gender. Once children begin to think about gender as a stable trait, they also start to incorporate gender into their own identity.

Around that time, they become motivated to relate to other members of their gender group and seek out gender-related information, often becoming strict about adhering to gender stereotypes.[4] For example, children between the ages of three and five prefer to play with members of their own gender. And they also prefer to engage with gender-stereo-typed toys and activities.

It isn't until a few years later—when they are between 7 and 10 years of age—that children become more relaxed about maintaining behaviors that are strictly male or female. It is around that age, for example, when both boys and girls might admit that they "like to play with trucks" or "like to play with dolls."[5]

Ahead of Their Time?

Recent media coverage of transgender people has drawn our attention back to the fact that while our chromosomes determine our sex, they are not the only factors that affect our gender identity. This is something that children seem to know early on but that most discard as they learn about basic anatomy and incorporate that information into their own gender identities. We often think of children's thinking as immature, but it may be that preschoolers are actually way ahead of their time.

Notes

1. Theresa M. Wizemann and Mary-Lou Pardue, eds. *Exploring the Biological Contributions to Human Health: Does Sex Matter?* (Washington, DC: National Academy Press, 2001), https://www.ncbi.nlm.nih.gov/books /NBK222297/.
2. Sandra Lipsitz Bem, "Genital Knowledge and Gender Constancy in Preschool Children," *Child Development* 60, no. 3 (1989), 649–62, https://doi.org/10.2307/1130730.
3. Diane N. Ruble, Lisa J. Taylor, Lisa Cyphers, Faith K. Greulich, Leah E. Lurye, and Patrick E. Shrout, "The Role of Gender Constancy in Early Gender Development," *Child Development* 78, no. 4 (2007): 1121–36, https://doi.org/10.1111/j.1467-8624.2007.01056.x.
4. Carol Lynn Martin and Diane Ruble, "Children's Search for Gender Cues: Cognitive Perspectives on Gender Development," *Current Directions in Psychological Science* 13, no. 2 (2004): 67–70, https://doi.org/10.1111 /j.0963-7214.2004.00276.x.
5. Hanns M. Trautner, Diane N. Ruble, Lisa Cyphers, Barbara Kirsten, Regina Behrendt, and Petra Hartmann, "Rigidity and Flexibility of Gender Stereotypes in Childhood: Developmental or Differential?," *Infant and Child Development: An International Journal of Research and Practice* 14, no. 4 (2005): 365–81, https://doi.org/10.1002/icd.399.

Chapter 13

How Parents Can Support a Child Who Comes Out as Trans

EM MATSUNO

YOUNG TRANSGENDER, or trans, people face high rates of anxiety, depression, and suicide. These elevated mental health risks largely stem from external factors—such as discrimination, victimization, and, most especially, family rejection—rather than from being trans.

When I was a research fellow at Palo Alto University, I developed and tested an online training program called the Parent Support Program to help parents better understand and support trans youth. Here I address how parents can be better advocates—and avoid common missteps—when their child identifies as trans or nonbinary.

What Are Common Challenges
That Parents with Trans Kids Face?

A big challenge for parents of trans kids is fear. Parents fear for their kid's safety. For example, they fear their kid will be bullied, so they may say, "No, I don't want you to wear that to school." Or if they don't have knowledge about trans identities, they may feel overwhelmed or not know what to do. And they worry about messing up themselves by saying or doing the wrong thing.

Another barrier is the beliefs and attitudes that parents may have. Parents may have grown up learning misconceptions about gender: for example, the belief that one's sex assigned at birth, which is typically based on anatomy, is the same thing as one's gender or the belief that gender is strictly male or female.

If extended family or their community is conservative, the parents themselves can experience rejection from others. People may tell them it's bad parenting if they let their kid transition. Sometimes parents have to risk being rejected by their loved ones, and it can put them in a difficult position as well.

What Does the Research Say about Parental Support?

A 2016 study showed that trans children who were supported by their parents had mental health outcomes similar to those of a cisgender control group.[1] Certainly, there have been other findings of trans youth having depression or suicidal ideation. As a result, some people think that being trans makes someone more likely to suffer from mental health risks. But really what we see is that it's not about being trans but about whether you're supported or not.[2]

One of the studies I worked on looked at different types of social support for trans youth: their friend/peer group, the trans community, and their family.[3] Of those three, family support had the strongest correlations with depression, anxiety, and resilience. It's unfortunate because a lot of trans people lose their family support and have to rely on others, but family has the greatest impact.

Online resources advise parents to support a trans child by using their chosen pronouns, advocating for them, educating themselves, and showing unconditional love. To this advice I would add something else important: parents, don't hesitate to get your own support.

A lot of times parents say they're 100 percent supportive

and accepting, and yet they still have negative feelings—
sadness or anxiety—and that's OK. It doesn't mean you're not
supportive. But sharing all your emotional difficulties with
your kid can make them feel like a burden or the cause of all
your distress. If parents can't find other parents in their local
community, there are online support groups. And get professional support if you can.

What Common Myths and Disinformation Are Most Troubling?

The main myth is "rapid onset gender dysphoria." It sounds
like a medical term, but it's not used in trans health whatsoever
and is based in faulty research. This myth often manifests
itself in the notion that "Oh my God, all of a sudden my child
is trans. They must be influenced by peers." A lot of time kids
reach puberty and then develop feelings of discomfort. Or
maybe it was happening before, but they weren't sharing it
with a parent, so it feels sudden to the parent but not to the
child.

Additionally, there's a lot of disinformation around gender-
affirming medical care, which is a big stressor for a lot of
parents. There's this fear: "What if they change their minds?"
Cases of regret after transitioning are extremely rare.[4] As for
puberty blockers, they are reversible and low-risk. Often, trans
people don't know what's right for them until they try some
things out.[5] Yes, there are risks to medical interventions, but

there are also significant risks associated with continued gender dysphoria: the discomfort a person can feel when their gender identity doesn't match their sex assigned at birth.

Why Are More Kids Today Identifying as Trans?

Trans and nonbinary people have been around for all of time, across all cultures and continents. So, it's not a new thing. But there's been an erasure of that history. Now there's more visibility and more acceptance, and younger generations are also learning earlier on about trans identities. They have what trans actress and activist Laverne Cox calls "possibility models," which let them think, "Oh, this is an option for me." For a lot of trans people my age or older, that wasn't a thing we knew about.

What Can Parents Say to Show Support When a Trans Child Comes Out?

Parents can recognize their kid's bravery and show gratitude by saying, "Thank you for letting me know." Also, explicitly say you love them. Trans kids fear rejection when coming out, so explicit support is important.

Common reactions are to say, "No, you're confused. You're just gay/lesbian. Are you sure?" Another is to ask too many questions, which kind of puts the kid on trial: "How did you know? When did you know?" When these questions are fired off in quick succession, the underlying message is "I don't believe you" or "I don't approve."

A better approach is to say, "Is it OK for me to ask some questions, or do you need some time?" Parents can also ask their kid, "How can I support you?" With younger kids, parents might give some examples: "Do you want me to use *he* when I refer to you, or not? What sounds good to you?"

Any Final Advice for Parents?

Learn to tolerate ambiguity, uncertainty, and fluidity. Parents often want to know who their child is going to be, with certainty, stability, and consistency. That rigidness comes from anxiety. But things won't always be clear. Allow your child to come to their own answers. Kids will need to do some exploration, so things may change. And that's OK. Openness from parents allows them to be who they are.

Notes

1. Kristina R. Olson, Lily Durwood, Madeleine DeMeules, and Katie A. McLaughlin, "Mental Health of Transgender Children Who Are Supported in Their Identities," *Pediatrics* 137, no. 3 (2016): e20153223, https://doi.org/10.1542/peds.2015-3223.
2. Maureen D. Connolly, Marcus J. Zervos, Charles J. Barone II, Christine C. Johnson, and Christine L. M. Joseph, "The Mental Health of Transgender Youth: Advances in Understanding," *Journal of Adolescent Health* 59, no. 5 (2016): 489–95, https://doi.org/10.1016/j.jadohealth.2016.06.012.
3. Jae A. Puckett, Emmie Matsuno, Christina Dyar, Brian Mustanski, and Michael E. Newcomb, "Mental Health and Resilience in Transgender Individuals: What Type of Support Makes a Difference?," *Journal of Family Psychology* 33, no. 8 (2019): 954–64, https://doi.org/10.1037/fam0000561.supp.
4. Chantal M. Wiepjes, Nienke M. Nota, Christel J. M. de Blok, Maartje Klaver, Annelou L. C. de Vries, S. Annelijn Wensing-Kruger, Renate T. de Jongh, et al., "The Amsterdam Cohort of Gender Dysphoria Study (1972–2015): Trends in Prevalence, Treatment, and Regrets," *Journal of Sexual Medicine* 15, no. 4 (2018): 582–90, https://doi.org/10.1016/j.jsxm.2018.01.016.
5. Florence Ashley, "Thinking an Ethics of Gender Exploration: Against Delaying Transition for Transgender and Gender Creative Youth," *Clinical Child Psychology and Psychiatry* 24, no. 2 (2019): 223–36, https://doi.org/10.1177/1359104519836462.

Chapter 14

How to Know
If Your Kid Is Transgender

TEY MEADOW

ARI HAD A DIFFICULT TIME talking about his gender. He had always been feminine, insisting on wearing only androgynous clothing, flowing pants in bright colors, patterned shirts, and scarves. His hair was long and carefully arranged, and his nails were usually painted with a kaleidoscope of colors. By the time he was 12, he vacillated between using male and female names and pronouns. At school he mostly socialized with female classmates, while performing in school plays and making art.

When I met his mother, Sandy, at an event for parents of transgender and nonbinary children, she spoke anxiously about his experience of puberty, his struggles with depression, and the daunting task of helping him cope with the changes in his body. Sandy read every parenting manual on gender nonconformity she could get her hands on. She wasn't sure whether Ari would grow up to be a gay man or a transgender woman, and she felt a tremendous amount of discomfort with that uncertainty.

Sandy was like many parents I met while doing research for *Trans Kids*, a book on families raising gender-nonconforming children.[1] These parents often struggled with the question of how to tell if their child was really transgender, merely experimenting with gender, or, instead, simply growing into an adolescent gay identity.

The Media Teaches Parents to Doubt

The parents and clinicians with whom I spoke all wished that there was some foolproof method to determine whether kids were actually transgender. They longed for a formula that would tell them, with certainty, that they could safely assist these kids with social and medical gender transition without fear of mistake or regret.

News articles and blog posts on the subject seem to appear weekly. In July 2018, for example, the *Atlantic* published a cover story about Claire, a gender-nonconforming 14-year-old. After a period of consideration, Claire decided that she didn't ultimately feel the need to transition. The author of that article, Jesse Singal, used Claire's experience to illustrate the complexities of parenting gender-diverse children.[2]

I found the article troubling, however, because it was a prime example of two dangerous trends in public discussions of parenting gender-nonconforming youth.

First, Claire's experience is not at all typical. The American Psychological Association found that children who "consistently, persistently and insistently" tell the adults around them that they are transgender almost never have a sudden and complete change of heart. Indeed, says the APA, gender identity is resistant—if not immutable—to environmental intervention.[3] Children can and do learn to *cover*, a term sociologists use for downplaying parts of one's identity to avoid negative reactions from other people. But that's different from no longer feeling transgender.

Second—and perhaps more important—the *Atlantic* article shifts the focus from whether a child might be transgender to asking how it might be possible for them not to be. This is called *cisnormativity*: the cultural belief that being gender normative is inherently better than being trans. And the media is, at times, its biggest proponent.

Stories and false statistics that exaggerate the proportion of children who stop exhibiting gender nonconformity may offer comfort to anxious parents who imagine cisgender life to be an easier path for their kids. But they also prompt those parents to interpret any signs of struggle or ambivalence as de facto evidence that their child is not trans, to withhold information about transgender lives from interested children, and to create an atmosphere in which children learn to hide the complexities of their experiences to garner the approval of adults.

Embracing Uncertainty

This is not a new story.

For decades, transgender adults have written about

their experiences seeking gender reassignment, describing how clinicians told them they needed to seem "authentically trans"—to report a total, unwavering identification with the other gender—to physicians and psychologists.[4] They had to exhibit an exclusive preference for clothing and activities consistent with the other gender, a heterosexual sexual orientation, and an ability to pass as a member of that gender. In short, they were held to the most rigid and restrictive social gender norms. Absent satisfying those criteria, trans people would be turned away from medical care and disbelieved by friends and family. As a result, many learned to cover up their ambivalences, struggles, and self-doubts. They learned to present a version of trans that seemed foolproof to cisgender people: a narrative in which gender is certain, in which it is impervious to the vicissitudes of actual emotional life.

This is not to say these trans people were uncertain about who they were. That's simply untrue. But self-knowledge rarely comes packaged in a single coherent narrative. And yet, this is the expectation we have of the children in our lives.

It's possible to do better. Development is not a linear process. It can weave through joy and ambivalence, through pain and delight. Adult gender doesn't come easily to anyone. It's fertile ground for self-doubt and humiliation, experimentation and adaptation.

Think for a moment about your own adolescence, the time when you experienced rapid bodily changes, social maturity, and emergent sexuality. Few of us remember this process as smooth and linear. Now imagine you had adults—perhaps even your parents—scrutinizing this process each step of the way and trying to nudge you toward fitting neatly into an identity or way of behaving that felt uncomfortable. This is a recipe for depression and anxiety in children. In anyone, really.

It doesn't have to be that way. Gender-nonconforming children who are supported by their parents in expressing their identities by and large thrive. In fact, studies show that trans youth who are affirmed and supported by their families in transitioning are psychologically healthier than children who are gender-nonconforming but receive no such encouragement.[5]

Moving from Knowing to Affirming

Dealing with uncertainty and ambivalence can be especially difficult for parents who fear their children will face discrimination in their communities. But, the truth is, it's difficult for all parents. As more families grapple with the complexities of gender development, we see stories of children and parents seeking guidance and support from clinicians who work from an affirmative model of care.[6]

This affirmative model doesn't push kids toward a transgender outcome or even a linear narrative. Instead, clinicians teach parents to pause, absorb the messages their children are sending, and then articulate what they are seeing back to their children. Parents and psychologists help children express their gender in authentic ways and then work to understand the significance of the things they are saying and doing. It takes time and practice. Affirmative clinical work treats all gender variations as potential signs of psychic health—not proof of psychiatric illness—and supports the unhurried unfolding of a child's emergent self.[7] In this context, uncertainty and ambivalence are a part of transgender development, just as they are for all gender development.

After some time and discussion, Sandy, Ari, and his therapist decided to put Ari on Lupon, one of a class of drugs used to suppress the body's production of the hormones that incite puberty. Sandy works hard to allow Ari to vacillate in his gender presentation and in his sense of self. When we last spoke, she told me she didn't know where he would end up. She knew there was no failsafe way to tell, only a process to go through. Whatever the conclusion, she told me, Ari knew that she was walking alongside him—but letting him lead the way.

Notes

1. Tey Meadow, *Trans Kids: Being Gendered in the Twenty-First Century* (Berkeley: University of California Press, 2018).
2. Jesse Singal, "When Children Say They're Trans: Hormones? Surgery? The Choices Are Fraught—and There Are No Easy Answers," *Atlantic*, July/August 2018, https://www.theatlantic.com/magazine/archive/2018/07/when-a-child-says-shes-trans/561749/.
3. Colt Meier and Julie Harris, *Fact Sheet: Gender Diversity and Transgender Identity in Children* (Washington, DC: American Psychological Association, n.d.), https://www.apadivisions.org/division-44/resources/advocacy/transgender-children.pdf.
4. Laura Erickson-Schroth, ed., *Trans Bodies, Trans Selves: A Resource by and for Transgender Communities*, 2nd ed. (Oxford: Oxford University Press, 2022).
5. Kristina R. Olson, Lily Durwood, Madeleine DeMeules, and Katie A. McLaughlin, "Mental Health of Transgender Children Who Are Supported in Their Identities," *Pediatrics* 137, no. 3 (2016): e20153223, https://doi.org/10.1542/peds.2015-3223.
6. Colt Keo-Meier and Diane Ehrensaft, eds. *The Gender Affirmative Model: An Interdisciplinary Approach to Supporting Transgender and Gender Expansive Children* (Washington, DC: American Psychological Association, 2018).
7. Diane Ehrensaft, "Found in Transition: Our Littlest Transgender People," *Contemporary Psychoanalysis* 50, no. 4 (2014): 571–92, https://doi.org/10.1080/00107530.2014.942591.

Chapter 15

7 Tips for LGBTQ Parents to Help Schools Fight Stigma and Ignorance

ABBIE E. GOLDBERG

MANY PARENTS WANT TO ENSURE that their kids are in classrooms where they and their families are respected and embraced. However, as a psychologist and researcher who has studied LGBTQ parents' relationships with schools for over a decade, I have found that LGBTQ parents often have specific concerns when it comes to inclusion and acceptance. "[We have] always been very up front that we are a family with two moms," reported one parent in my research. "If the [school] was going to have an issue, we wanted to get the vibe early so we could find an alternative so our child didn't have to suffer due to their closed-mindedness." LGBTQ parents who live in less gay-friendly communities are more likely to describe feelings of mistreatment by their children's schools.[1] Such experiences may prompt parents to confront negative treatment.[2]

Based on my research and surveys with hundreds of LGBTQ families, here are seven suggestions for how LGBTQ caregivers can advocate for themselves and their children if they run into stigma or ignorance. The statements quoted below are from various participants in my research.

1. **Talk to the school preemptively.**

"I always tell the teachers in advance that I am a transgender gestational parent so they don't think my kids are lying when they say their father gave birth to them."

Engage the school in a conversation about your family prior to the start of the school year. Explain the basic details of your family, including what your child calls each parent and other important adults in your child's life such as a donor or birth parents. Ask school administrators or teachers if they have any questions or would like you to suggest some resources.

2. **Get involved.**

"My presence in these spaces is a constant reminder to the staff that there is a gay parent in the room."

Join the school's PTA (parent-teacher association) or diversity committee, or attend their meetings and gradually seek out leadership positions. Volunteer in the classroom or at school events.

3. **Provide input and suggestions.**

"We bought books for the class library about different kinds of families and arranged for PFLAG [a national advocacy group organized by the families of LGBTQ people] and local LGBTQ groups to present to staff at our kids' schools."

Highlight for schools where paperwork can be more inclusive, such as "Parent 1" and "Parent 2" instead of "Mother" and "Father." Provide input about how celebrations, curriculum, and classroom visuals could be more inclusive of families with LGBTQ parents or donate inclusive books or other materials.

4. **Investigate policies.**

Establish whether the school has procedures in place for dealing with sexist, homophobic, and transphobic behavior at school. What are the school's policies against bullying? If sexual and gender identity and expression are not covered in such policies, advocate for including them.

5. **Talk to your children.**

"We have told them that every family is different . . . We told them that some people don't understand these differences and to feel free to come to us at any time if they have questions."

Check in with your children about what they are experiencing at school. Use general questions or prompts, such as "What is your teacher like?" or "Tell me about recess today." Convey that you'll listen to them if something is going on at school and that you'll talk together about how to handle it.

6. **Empower your children.**

"There's a lot of 'That's gay' or 'You're gay.' When someone says to my daughter, 'Your mom's gay,' she says, 'Actually, she is.'"

Build your child's confidence and sense of pride. If possible, connect them to other children with LGBTQ parents. This can make a difference in terms of their self-esteem.[3] Help them develop a repertoire of potential responses to teasing—such as telling a teacher, ignoring it, or responding to an insensitive question with a straightforward set of facts. Consider outlining or role-playing possible scenarios.

7. **Get support.**

    "We did a presentation to the first-grade class . . . With the school's permission, we shared how our family was created, and other parents joined in and shared their stories as well so as not to single out our son."

    Find a community of other LGBTQ parents at school, in your community, or online. You may also find allies in non-LGBTQ parents who want diverse and inclusive schools.

Benefits of Inclusive Schools

Research has shown that attending schools where LGBTQ topics and historical figures are incorporated into the curriculum, or where there are supports for LGBTQ people, benefits the mental health and self-esteem of children with LGBTQ parents.[4] Having classmates who also have LGBTQ parents can help too. Furthermore, children with LGBTQ parents who attend LGBTQ-inclusive schools may be less likely to experience bullying than those who attend schools with more negative environments.[5] One study found that children of LGBTQ parents who attended schools without LGBTQ issues in the curriculum showed higher levels of withdrawn and aggressive behavior, along with more social problems.[6]

Undoubtedly, LGBTQ parents should also consider a school's quality and reputation, class sizes, safety, and ability to meet their children's needs and interests.

In seeking out inclusive schools and advocating for their children, LGBTQ parents should be sure to give themselves a break. It is impossible to fight or win every battle, and in a just world, LGBTQ parents would not have to fight these battles at all.

Notes

1. Abbie E. Goldberg and JuliAnna Z. Smith, "Preschool Selection Considerations and Experiences of School Mistreatment among Lesbian, Gay, and Heterosexual Adoptive Parents," *Early Childhood Research Quarterly* 29, no. 1 (2014): 64–75, https://doi.org/10.1016/j.ecresq.2013.09.006.
2. Abbie E. Goldberg, Kaitlin Black, Kristin Sweeney, and April Moyer, "Lesbian, Gay, and Heterosexual Adoptive Parents' Perceptions of Inclusivity and Receptiveness in Early Childhood Education Settings," *Journal of Research in Childhood Education* 31, no. 1 (2017), 141–59, https://doi.org/10.1080/02568543.2016.1244136.
3. Henny M. W. Bos and Frank Van Balen, "Children in Planned Lesbian Families: Stigmatisation, Psychological Adjustment and Protective Factors," *Culture, Health & Sexuality* 10, no. 3 (2008): 221–36. https://doi.org/10.1080/13691050701601702.
4. Johanna D. Vyncke, Danielle Julien, Emilie Jouvin, and Emilie Jodoin, "Systemic Heterosexism and Adjustment among Adolescents Raised by Lesbian Mothers," *Canadian Journal of Behavioural Science / Revue canadienne des sciences du comportement* 46, no. 3 (2014): 375–86, https://doi.org/10.1037/a0034663.
5. Abbie E. Goldberg and Randi Garcia, "Community Characteristics, Victimization, and Psychological Adjustment among School-Aged Adopted Children with Lesbian, Gay, and Heterosexual Parents," *Frontiers in Psychology* 11 (2020): 372, https://doi.org/10.3389/fpsyg.2020.00372.
6. Henny M. W. Bos, Nanette K. Gartrell, Heidi Peyser, and Frank van Balen, "The USA National Longitudinal Lesbian Family Study (NLLFS): Homophobia, Psychological Adjustment, and Protective Factors," *Journal of Lesbian Studies* 12, no. 4 (2008): 455–71, https://doi.org/10.1080/10894160802278630.

Chapter 16

Nearly 10 Percent of Youth in One Urban School District Identify as Gender-Diverse

KACIE KIDD

IT SEEMS THAT MORE AND MORE teens are identifying as transgender, gender-fluid, or nonbinary. But because linguistic and cultural norms are always evolving, it's been challenging to pin down an exact number.

The 2017 Youth Risk Behavior Survey, which was conducted by the Centers for Disease Control and Prevention, found that 1.8 percent of high school students identified as transgender.[1] But my team—made up of pediatricians, adolescent medicine specialists, and public health researchers—

suspected that this study underrepresented the prevalence of gender-diverse youth. That's because not all people who are gender-diverse, an umbrella term for those whose gender identity does not fully align with the sex they were assigned at birth, identify as "transgender."

So, we put together a survey using more inclusive questions. We asked high school students in Pittsburgh questions about their gender in two steps. First, we asked about their sex assigned at birth. Then we asked about their gender identity and allowed them to select the identities that applied to them.

The results of our survey were published in 2021.[2] Of the 3,168 teens who answered the questions, 9.2 percent had a gender identity that did not fully align with their sex assigned at birth. For example, someone assigned female at birth might identify with a gender other than "girl," such as "nonbinary," "boy," or "trans boy." This was a larger proportion than we'd seen in prior studies. And it may be that our inclusive questions, which allowed us to identify anyone whose sex and gender identity did not fully align, ultimately reflect the true prevalence of gender-diverse people.

There were some other notable findings.

For one, we found that more teens of color expressed gender-diverse identities than their white counterparts. Yet the pediatric gender clinic in Pittsburgh, like similar clinics

across the United States, sees white patients predominantly.[3] Reasons for this pattern are not fully known, but we suspect that gender-diverse communities of color may have less access to medical specialists. They may also experience increased stigma and discrimination for being both nonwhite and gender-diverse.

We also found that among the teens who identified as gender-diverse in our survey, more expressed a feminine or nonbinary identity, which doesn't reflect the makeup of the patients seen in both our local clinic and in gender-care clinics across the country, where patients tend to express masculine identities.[4] This may be because trans women and girls—particularly trans women and girls of color—face higher rates of violence and so may be less comfortable coming out and seeking care.[5]

There are also mental health implications for these gender-diverse young people. On average, teens with gender-diverse identities have higher rates of depression and thoughts of suicide compared with their peers who are cisgender, that is, those who identify with the sex they were assigned at birth.[6] The higher rates may be associated with gender dysphoria: the distress associated with an incongruence between sex assigned at birth and gender identity. Not all gender-diverse people have gender dysphoria, but those who do may benefit from gender-affirming care.[7]

My experience in caring for this population of young people was substantiated by the numbers we saw from this survey: gender-diverse teens exist—and in larger numbers than many people might realize. Their lives and experiences matter, and given the fact that they're more vulnerable to mental health concerns, I believe equal access to compassionate, comprehensive health care becomes that much more crucial.

Notes

1. Michelle M. Johns, Richard Lowry, Jack Andrzejewski, Lisa C. Barrios, Zewditu Demissie, Timothy McManus, Catherine N. Rasberry, Leah Robin, and J. Michael Underwood, "Transgender Identity and Experiences of Violence Victimization, Substance Use, Suicide Risk, and Sexual Risk Behaviors among High School Students—19 States and Large Urban School Districts," *Morbidity and Mortality Weekly Report* 68, no. 3 (2019): 67–71, https://doi.org/10.15585/mmwr.mm6803a3.
2. Kacie M. Kidd, Gina M. Sequeira, Claudia Douglas, Taylor Paglisotti, David J. Inwards-Breland, Elizabeth Miller, and Robert W. S. Coulter, "Prevalence of Gender-Diverse Youth in an Urban School District," *Pediatrics* 147, no. 6 (2021): e2020049823, https://doi.org/10.1542/peds.2020-049823.
3. Gina M. Sequeira, Kristin N. Ray, Elizabeth Miller, and Robert W. S. Coulter, "Transgender Youth's Disclosure of Gender Identity to Providers outside of Specialized Gender Centers," *Journal of Adolescent Health* 66, no. 6 (2020): 691–98, https://doi.org/10.1016/j.jadohealth.2018.10.101.

4. Melinda Chen, John Fuqua, and Erica A. Eugster, "Characteristics of Referrals for Gender Dysphoria over a 13-Year Period," *Journal of Adolescent Health* 58, no. 3 (2016): 369–71, https://doi.org/10.1016/j.jadohealth.2015.11.010.

5. Robert Garofalo, Joanne Deleon, Elizabeth Osmer, Mary Doll, and Gary W. Harper, "Overlooked, Misunderstood and At-Risk: Exploring the Lives and HIV Risk of Ethnic Minority Male-to-Female Transgender Youth," *Journal of Adolescent Health* 38, no. 3 (2006): 230–36, https://doi.org/10.1016/j.jadohealth.2005.03.023.

6. Johns et al., "Transgender Identity."

7. Eli Coleman, "Standards of Care for the Health of Transsexual, Transgender, and Gender-Nonconforming People," in *Principles of Gender-Specific Medicine*, 3rd ed., ed. Marianne J. Legato (Cambridge, MA: Academic Press, 2017), 69–75, https://doi.org/10.1016/b978-0-12-803506-1.00058-9.

Chapter 17

5 Ways Parents Can Help Kids Avoid Gender Stereotypes

KYL MYERS

OVER THE PAST CENTURY, significant progress has been made in advancing gender equity in the United States. Women gained the right to vote, fathers have become more involved parents, and more people and institutions recognize gender identities beyond the binary categories of male and female.[1] However, persistent gaps remain. Women hold only a quarter of US congressional seats, only a handful of states mandate paid paternity leave, and state legislatures are introducing bills that discriminate against transgender people.

The majority of Americans believe there is more work to

do on gender equality. As a genderqueer sociologist, a parent, and the author of a book on gender-creative parenting, I study the importance of disrupting sexism in childhood. Here are five ways I've found that parents and caregivers can fight gender stereotypes in kids' lives.

1. Acknowledge that a child may be LGBTQI+

Gender identity and sexuality are diverse and personal experiences. However, medical institutions and parents commonly assign a sex to newborns based on physical characteristics and then socialize children as one of two binary genders. For example, children with vulvas are assigned female and raised as girls and children with penises are assigned male and raised as boys.

Many children are cisgender—meaning their gender identity aligns with the sex and gender they were assigned at birth. However, the percentage of young people in the United States who are transgender—meaning their gender does not align with the sex they were assigned at birth—is growing. So too is the number who are nonbinary—meaning their gender is neither strictly male or female. And an estimated 1 in every 1,500 to 2,000 babies born in the United States is intersex— meaning their sex chromosomes or reproductive anatomy is different from what is typically categorized male or female.[2]

Additionally, nationwide, more than 11 percent of high school students say they are lesbian, gay, bisexual, or questioning their sexuality.[3] Young LGBTQ people are coming out to their families earlier than older generations did. Research shows that family acceptance of young LGBTQ people is associated with greater mental and physical health and protection against depression, substance abuse, and suicide.[4]

2. Be Aware of Gendered Marketing

Children's toys and clothes are increasingly divided by gender, and many people blame the profit-driven exploitation of gender-stereotyped marketing.[5] For example, building toys and small vehicles are marketed to boys, and dolls and makeup to girls. In children's clothing stores, primary colors and transportation and sport graphics are often on one side, while pastels, flowers, and sparkles are on the other.

Children learn important social, emotional, and physical life skills through play. Playing with a variety of toys provides opportunities to develop and build on well-rounded skills, including spatial awareness and empathy. Gender-stereotyped marketing can limit the kinds of toys and experiences children are exposed to.

Parents and caregivers can shop all the aisles of a toy or clothing store to show children that gendered marketing boundaries are arbitrary and can be crossed. They can let kids explore what is available and choose for themselves.

Counterstereotyping—explicitly reversing a stereotype— is another powerful way to disrupt gender stereotypes in play. For example, a caregiver can look at dolls with a boy and say things like "Boys like dolls" and "Daddies are really good at caring for babies."

3. Disrupt Gender Stereotypes at Home

Parents and caregivers are children's first models for how gender is performed. Adults can model language and behavior that challenge binary and harmful sexist stereotypes, such as the belief that women should do more housework, even when they have full-time employment. For example, in households with more than one parent, and especially in different-gender couples, parents can share parenting responsibilities and household tasks. Actions speak louder than words, and children are more likely to reject the idea of traditional gender norms when their parents exhibit fairness and divide domestic labor equitably, not just mention it as something they value.

Parents can switch up children's chores so that they learn about housekeeping in a nongendered way. Boys can do dishes, and girls can take out the garbage. Parents can also ensure their children's allowance is equitable, as the gender pay gap can start at home. Research suggests girls earn less allowance even when they do more chores.[6]

4. Use Gender-Neutral Language

Using gender-neutral pronouns and other words can reduce gender bias and increase positive regard for women and LGBT people.[7] For example, using anatomical language instead of gendered words, such as *vulva* instead of *girl parts*, teaches children that not all people who have vulvas identify as girls. This doesn't erase cisgender girls but is inclusive of many transgender boys and nonbinary kids. Similarly, replacing *moms and dads* with *parents and caregivers* is not only inclusive of same-sex and nonbinary parents but also acknowledges single parents as well as grandparents and nonrelative guardians.

In children's books, where boy characters far outnumber girls and other genders, caregivers can change he/him pronouns to she/her and they/them. Adults can also choose books and media that represent kids in diverse and inclusive ways and call out stereotypes when they come up in stories.

5. Encourage Mixed-Gender Play

Gender segregation is deeply embedded in social structures and can have negative implications, such as sexist attitudes toward people of other genders. Children are often categorized in gendered groups, sometimes casually ("boys line up here; girls line up there") and other times explicitly, as in single-sex schools.

Research shows that children who have close friendships with children of other genders hold more positive and less sexist attitudes toward their friend's gender.[8] Parents and educators can create opportunities for kids to interact with children of different genders. They can stop segregating children by gender, choose sports teams and other organized extracurricular activities that are open to all genders, and host mixed-gender birthday parties, for example. All-gender activities help children recognize their similarities and celebrate their differences and are inclusive of children who don't identify as a girl or boy.

Notes

1. Nicole Elias and Roddrick Colvin, "A Third Option: Understanding and Assessing Non-binary Gender Policies in the United States," *Administrative Theory & Praxis* 42, no. 2 (2020): 191–211, https://doi.org/10.1080/10841806.2019.1659046.
2. Georgiann Davis and Sharon Preves, "Intersex and the Social Construction of Sex," *Contexts* 16, no. 1 (2017): 80, https://doi.org/10.1177/1536504217696082.
3. Laura Kann, Emily O'Malley Olsen, Tim McManus, William A. Harris, Shari L. Shanklin, Katherine H. Flint, Barbara Queen, et al., "Sexual Identity, Sex of Sexual Contacts, and Health-Related Behaviors among Students in Grades 9–12—United States and Selected Sites, 2015," *Morbidity and Mortality Weekly Report: Surveillance Summaries* 65, no. SS-9 (August 12, 2016): 1–202. https://doi.org/10.15585/mmwr.ss6509a1.
4. Caitlin Ryan, Stephen T. Russell, David Huebner, Rafael Diaz, and Jorge Sanchez, "Family Acceptance in Adolescence and the Health of LGBT

Young Adults," *Journal of Child and Adolescent Psychiatric Nursing* 23, no. 4 (2010): 205–13, https://doi.org/10.1111/j.1744-6171.2010.00246.x.

5. Carol J. Auster and Claire S. Mansbach, "The Gender Marketing of Toys: An Analysis of Color and Type of Toy on the Disney Store Website," *Sex Roles* 67, nos. 7–8 (2012): 375–88, https://doi.org/10.1007/s11199-012-0177-8.

6. Renee Morad, "The Gender Pay Gap Starts Earlier Than You Think," MSNBC, October 29, 2018, https://www.msnbc.com/know-your-value/gender-pay-gap-starts-earlier-you-think-n925696.

7. Margit Tavits and Efrén O. Pérez, "Language Influences Mass Opinion toward Gender and LGBT Equality," *Proceedings of the National Academy of Sciences* 116, no. 34 (2019): 16781–86, https://doi.org/10.1073/pnas.1908156116.

8. Zosuls, and Diane N. Ruble, "Enjoying Each Other's Company: Gaining Other-Gender Friendships Promotes Positive Gender Attitudes among Ethnically Diverse Children," *Personality and Social Psychology Bulletin* 47 (12): 1635–53, https://doi.org/10.1177/0146167220984407.

Chapter 18

How to Tell If Your College Is Trans-Inclusive

ABBIE E. GOLDBERG

HIGH SCHOOL can be especially challenging for US teens who identify as transgender, or trans. They disproportionately experience harassment and victimization by their peers and rejection by family members.[1] Entering a trans-affirming and gender-inclusive college environment can help set trans youth on a path of personal, academic, and professional success. A trans-affirming college can also be transformative for trans students who did not feel comfortable being out in high school, as well as those who do not begin to explore their gender identity until college.

My research from 2018 with 507 trans and gender-nonconforming students—75 percent undergraduate, 25 percent graduate—examined which college policies and supports trans students valued the most. I also looked at how these policies created a sense of belonging on campus.[2] I found that religiously affiliated colleges and community colleges tended to be less inclusive of trans students. Also, knowing that a school had trans-inclusive policies and supports led to a greater feeling of belonging and a better perception of the campus climate. As the supports they valued most, students identified gender-inclusive restrooms, nondiscrimination policies that cover gender identity, and the ability to easily change one's name on campus records.

Based on these findings, I offer a few key things that trans students and their families may want to consider in the college exploration process.

Gender-Inclusive Restrooms

Trans students can look for whether most campus buildings—especially those with heavy traffic, such as the campus student center—have gender-inclusive restrooms. These may also be called gender-neutral or all-gender restrooms. Bonus points go to institutions whose gender-inclusive restrooms have multiple stalls to accommodate more people and to those that have committed to constructing gender-inclusive restrooms in all new buildings. Athletic facilities, meanwhile, ideally have private changing facilities and private showers.

This kind of systemic inclusion can support students' mental health and academic achievement. For example, one study found that not having access to inclusive and comfortable restrooms was associated with poorer academic performance.[3]

Gender-Inclusive Housing

Gender-inclusive housing refers to students' freedom to be housed in keeping with their gender identity and to choose whom to room with—among returning students, at least—regardless of gender. Campus Pride, a nonprofit network of LGBTQ student leaders and campus groups, found that, as of January 2022, at least 425 colleges and universities in the United States had gender-inclusive housing.[4]

Nondiscrimination Policies

Prospective students may want to look at schools' non-discrimination policies to make sure they explicitly include gender identity and expression. Such policies protect trans students from discrimination on the basis of gender identity and expression, and they symbolize an institution's commitment to fairness and equity.

Chosen Name and Pronouns Options

Prospective students may also want to investigate whether prospective schools allow students to use a chosen first name, instead of their legal name, on campus records, identification cards, course rosters, and other documents.

Health and Counseling Services

Campus health care centers may or may not serve trans students' needs, such as prescribing and overseeing hormone treatments. Likewise, trans students should find out whether student health insurance covers trans-affirming medical care. Campus Pride reported that, as of January 2022, 89 colleges and universities covered hormones and gender-affirming surgeries in their student health insurance plans, while 23 covered hormones alone.[5]

According to the Cooperative Institutional Research Program Freshman Survey, incoming trans college students tend to report poorer emotional health than their cisgender, or cis, peers[6] (meaning their gender identity aligns with their assigned sex at birth). Trans students are also more likely to anticipate seeking counseling while in college. Therefore it may be important that the student counseling center be explicitly inclusive of trans people. This means, for example, having a counselor who identifies as trans or at least one who is trained on the needs and experiences of trans people.

Affinity Groups

Prospective students can also find out whether there is a campus LGBTQ student center or group, ideally with affiliate groups or clubs—for example, for trans students or queer students of color. Groups that are more niche, though, may be harder to find at smaller institutions.

Training on Gender Identity

Some institutions offer or require training on gender identity and the experiences of trans people for their staff, faculty, and even students, such as peer advisers and student orientation leaders. The level of awareness a campus community has about trans issues and people is closely related to classroom and campus climate for trans students.

My research has found that nonbinary students—those whose gender identities lie outside the male/female gender binary, as opposed to trans men and trans women—also face challenges in college.[7] They report chronic misgendering, or being referred to as she/her or he/him instead of they/them, as well as an inability to represent themselves accurately on forms and paperwork.

Coursework and Research Opportunities

Students may also be interested in examining whether faculty teach courses that are trans-inclusive and -affirming, such as trans history or trans literature. They can also check to see whether a school has faculty research centers that focus on trans experiences.

Financial and Material Support

Trans students often enter college with more financial concerns than their cis peers. These may relate to hormone treatments and gender-confirmation surgeries in addition to funding their college education. Furthermore, trans students are more likely to report needing to work full-time during college and receiving more financial aid than cis students.

Some schools have an emergency fund for trans students in need of basic assistance or have other free on-campus resources such as "clothing closets" for trans and gender-nonconforming students.

Other Questions to Ask

A number of other markers of trans inclusion can be harder to immediately assess.

Prospective students can ask tour guides and student ambassadors whether there are any trans people in student government, what is the overall climate for trans students, and whether campus events include issues of interest to trans students and even feature invited trans speakers. Other features to look for are campus task forces or committees that address and include trans people, the presence of trans faculty and staff, and specialized student orientation content or modules for trans students.

It may also be possible to be connected to current trans students or recent alumni to hear about their experiences at the school and to ask whether there is anything else a prospective trans student should know.

Notes

1. Michelle M. Johns, Richard Lowry, Jack Andrzejewski, Lisa C. Barrios, Zewditu Demissie, Timothy McManus, Catherine N. Rasberry, Leah Robin, and J. Michael Underwood, "Transgender Identity and Experiences of Violence Victimization, Substance Use, Suicide Risk, and Sexual Risk Behaviors among High School Students—19 States and Large Urban School Districts, 2017," *Morbidity and Mortality Weekly Report* 68, no. 3 (2019): 67–71, https://doi.org/10.15585/mmwr.mm6803a3; Emily M. Pariseau, Lydia Chevalier, Kristin A. Long, Rebekah Clapham, Laura Edwards-Leeper, and Amy C. Tishelman, "The Relationship between Family Acceptance-Rejection and Transgender Youth Psychosocial Functioning," *Clinical Practice in Pediatric Psychology* 7, no. 3 (2019): 267–77, https://doi.org/10.1037/cpp0000291.
2. Abbie E. Goldberg, Genny Beemyn, and JuliAnna Z. Smith, "What Is Needed, What Is Valued: Trans Students' Perspectives on Trans-Inclusive Policies and Practices in Higher Education," *Journal of Educational and Psychological Consultation* 29, no. 1 (2018): 27–67, https://doi.org/10.1080/10474412.2018.1480376.
3. Michael R. Woodford, Jessica Y. Joslin, Erich N. Pitcher, and Kristen A. Renn, "A Mixed-Methods Inquiry into Trans* Environmental Microaggressions on College Campuses: Experiences and Outcomes," *Journal of Ethnic & Cultural Diversity in Social Work* 26, nos. 1–2 (2017): 95–111, https://doi.org/10.1080/15313204.2016.1263817.
4. "Colleges and University That Provide Gender-Inclusive Housing," Campus Pride, https://www.campuspride.org/tpc/gender-inclusive-housing/.

5. "Colleges and Universities That Cover Transition-Related Medical Expenses under Student Health Insurance," Campus Pride, https://www.campuspride.org/tpc/student-health-insurance/.

6. Ellen Bara Stolzenberg and Bryce Hughes, "The Experiences of Incoming Transgender College Students: New Data on Gender Identity," *Liberal Education* 103, no. 2 (2017), https://eric.ed.gov/?id=EJ1150803.

7. Abbie E. Goldberg, Katherine A. Kuvalanka, Stephanie L. Budge, Madeline B. Benz, and JuliAnna Z. Smith, "Health Care Experiences of Transgender Binary and Nonbinary University Students," *Counseling Psychologist* 47, no. 1 (2019): 59–97, https://doi.org/10.1177/0011000019827568.

Chapter 19

Transgender Youth on Puberty Blockers and Gender-Affirming Hormones Have Lower Odds of Depression and Suicidal Thoughts, a Study Finds

DIANA M. TORDOFF and ARIN COLLIN

ONE STUDY ESTIMATED that 1.8 percent,[1] another that 2.7 percent[2] (or approximately 750,000 to 1.1 million), of adolescents in the United States identify as transgender or nonbinary. Many of these trans youth experience high levels of negative mental health symptoms owing to anti-transgender stigma, discrimination, and a lack of family or peer support. A 2021 study found that as much as 72 percent of trans youth were depressed, and half had seriously considered suicide.[3]

We are an epidemiologist and a medical student who
study ways to make clinical care more inclusive for trans and
nonbinary people. We conducted a study in collaboration with
the Seattle Children's Hospital Gender Clinic and found that
transgender youth on puberty blockers and gender-affirming
hormone therapy were less likely to report depression and
suicidal thoughts.[4]

Safe and Proven Treatments

Puberty blockers are medications that delay puberty. By
temporarily stopping the body from making the hormones
that lead to puberty-related changes, young people and their
families are given time to pause and make health decisions.
These medications have been used for over 30 years to treat
young people with puberty that starts too early, also called
precocious puberty.[5]

Gender-affirming hormone therapy, such as with testosterone or estrogen, provides medications that allow trans
youth to experience a puberty appropriately aligned with their
gender.

There is no shortage of scientific and clinical societies
that have found these medications to be both safe and
effective for transgender people. Numerous medical and
professional societies, including the American Academy of
Pediatrics, the American Academy of Child and Adolescent
Psychiatry, and the American Medical Association, endorse

access to gender-affirming care specifically for trans youth. Social support, as well as access to gender-affirming care, is known to significantly reduce poor mental health in trans youth. In addition, several studies have suggested that early access to puberty blockers and hormones during adolescence can have long-term positive effects that last into adulthood. Despite these benefits, many young people face significant barriers to accessing gender-affirming care. Only one in five youth who need hormones has been able to access them.[6]

To further examine the mental health effects of puberty blockers and hormone therapy, we followed 104 trans and nonbinary youth ages 13 to 20 during their first year of gender-affirming care. After one year, we found that young people who began puberty blockers or gender-affirming hormones were 60 percent less likely to be depressed and 73 percent less likely to have thoughts about self-harm or suicide compared with youth who hadn't started these medications.

In addition, young people who were unable to start these medications within three to six months of their first appointment with a medical provider had a two- to threefold increase in depression and suicidal thoughts. Our findings suggest that delays in prescribing hormones and puberty blockers may worsen mental health symptoms for trans youth.

What This Means for Anti-transgender Legislation

The years 2021 and 2022 were record-breaking ones for anti-transgender legislation, including attempts to criminalize gender-affirming care for trans youth.[7] Banning gender-affirming care will have immediate and long-term negative effects on the well-being of trans youth and their families, both by increasing the stigma and discrimination these young people face and by denying them access to lifesaving and evidence-based health care. Our study builds on existing scientific evidence and affirms that timely access to gender-affirming care saves trans youths' lives.

Notes

1. Michelle M. Johns, Richard Lowry, Jack Andrzejewski, Lisa C. Barrios, Zewditu Demissie, Timothy McManus, Catherine N. Rasberry, Leah Robin, and J. Michael Underwood, "Transgender Identity and Experiences of Violence Victimization, Substance Use, Suicide Risk, and Sexual Risk Behaviors among High School Students—19 States and Large Urban School Districts, 2017," *Morbidity and Mortality Weekly Report* 68, no. 3 (2019): 67–71, https://doi.org/10.15585/mmwr.mm6803a3.
2. Marla E. Eisenberg, Amy L. Gower, Barbara J. McMorris, Nicole Rider, Glynis Shea, and Eli Coleman, "Risk and Protective Factors in the Lives of Transgender / Gender Nonconforming Adolescents, *Journal of Adolescent Health* 61, no. 4 (2017): 521–26, https://doi.org/10.1016/j.jadohealt.2017.04.014.
3. Amy E. Green, Jonah P. DeChants, Myeshia N. Price, and Carrie K. Davis, "Association of Gender-Affirming Hormone Therapy with Depression,

Thoughts of Suicide, and Attempted Suicide among Transgender and Nonbinary Youth," *Journal of Adolescent Health* 70, no. 4 (2022): 643–49, https://doi.org/10.1016/j.jadohealth.2021.10.036.

4. Diana M. Tordoff, Jonathon W. Wanta, Arin Collin, Cesalie Stepney, David J. Inwards-Breland, and Kym Ahrens, "Mental Health Outcomes in Transgender and Nonbinary Youths Receiving Gender-Affirming Care," *JAMA Network Open* 5, no. 2 (2022): e220978, https://doi.org/10.1001/jamanetworkopen.2022.0978.

5. Eun Young Kim, "Long-Term Effects of Gonadotropin-Releasing Hormone Analogs in Girls with Central Precocious Puberty," *Korean Journal of Pediatrics* 58, no. 1 (2015): 1–7, https://doi.org/10.3345/kjp.2015.58.1.1.

6. Green et al., "Association of Gender-Affirming Hormone Therapy."

7. Jack L. Turban, Katherine L. Kraschel, and Glenn Cohen, "Legislation to Criminalize Gender-Affirming Medical Care for Transgender Youth," *JAMA* 325, no. 22 (2021): 2251, https://doi.org/10.1001/jama.2021.7764.

Part IV.

Transgender Health Care and Medicine

The conversation around trans and nonbinary people has largely been framed through a medical lens. In fact, even though to be trans is no longer considered a psychiatric condition, the idea of being trans is still tied overwhelmingly in the public mind to both physical and psychological medicine. Medications, chiefly puberty blockers or hormones, and surgeries are often invoked as though they were the key to understanding trans people—or to deciding their human rights. At worst, conspiracy theorists and anti-trans groups peddle the idea that trans people are literal inventions of medicine. At best, discussions of trans and nonbinary people often begin by suggesting that they suffer from high rates of depression and anxiety or that they experience a higher risk of suicide. Regardless of the form it takes, the pervasive medical association itself requires some explanation. How did medicine come to be the primary lens through which trans people are viewed, and what does this conventional framing leave out?

While transgender medicine is often perceived as a new and under-researched specialty, it has existed for over a century. And while the recent politicization of trans medicine can make doctors and other health care providers appear like the natural allies of trans people, there are lively and unresolved debates among activists and providers about how to expand access to care by making gender affirmation a routine part of general medical practice. Some trans activists push to de-pathologize trans medicine altogether as a part of liberating trans people from institutions, such as health care, that harm them. Indeed, the medications, surgeries, and forms of care that trans people need access to are all routinely made available to non-trans people in like or identical form. The difference in accessibility and stigma, however, is nothing short of staggering.

A trans woman in the United States who wants her private insurance to cover an orchiectomy, for instance, might need two outside letters from psychiatric and medical doctors testifying to her conformity with the diagnosis of gender dysphoria in addition to the endorsement of her urologist. In essence, providers who have no familiarity with her life or health—including a mental health provider who has no expertise in urology—get to decide whether she deserves the procedure. Obtaining those letters can also cost several hundred dollars. A cisgender man, meanwhile, might be cleared for the same surgery by a simple diagnosis of "testicular pain" from the same urologist, with no additional steps required. The surgery is, in both cases, the same, which begs a larger question: What if the most meaningful difference between transgender medicine and non-transgender medicine is *transphobia*?

The chapters in part IV are broadly concerned with what are called the social determinants of health: the discrimination, stigma, and material obstacles that continue to prevent trans people from receiving competent, accessible health care. The contributors detail how health care discrimination is rampant for trans and nonbinary people in the United States, how providers themselves are often driven by anxiety over what they don't understand, how conversion therapy continues to inflict harm, and how the existing state of transgender medicine is creating divisions between those who have access to transition and those who do not. The root concern in any discussion of trans medicine ought to be this basic fact: that most trans people do not have access to the health care they want and need. And to see these important chapters in context, it's helpful to know first how that situation arose. Where did trans medicine come from, how was it initially organized to harm trans people, and how recent—and, consequently, fragile—is today's gender-affirming care model?

Another difficulty in any discussion of "transgender medicine" is that there is no such uniform thing behind the phrase. Although there are international organizations that publish standards of care, such as the World Professional Association for Transgender Health, there is no corresponding data set available on *how* (or whether) standards of care are actually implemented.[1] So much, then, depends on variations in national context, where laws, funding mechanisms, public versus private insurance, and cultural norms all differ. There is also a global economy of health care tourism for wealthy, mostly Western trans people that has a long history of facilitating access to surgeries for those who can pay.[2] And even within the United States, for example, the patchwork of the private health care landscape, with different state laws, federal regulations, and insurance plans, makes for a dizzying array of variation. That is all before we even consider that the clinical delivery of trans medicine varies widely from provider to provider.

Nevertheless, the history of transgender medicine does provide a clear picture of different stages of organization, access, and harm. The United States was a late adopter of a medical model first put forth in Western Europe, especially in Germany and Denmark. The famous Institut für Sexualwissenschaft, founded in 1919 in Berlin by the sexologist and social reformer Magnus Hirschfeld, was one of the first clinical spaces dedicated to trans people in the Western world. Hirschfeld was part of a burgeoning international and colonial scientific and medical field interested in sex and sexuality. Some of the first gender-affirming surgeries in Europe were arranged through Hirschfeld, who coined the term *transvestite* in 1910 to distinguish trans people from gay and lesbian people. The fascist tide rising in Europe in the 1930s proved to be cataclysmic for Hirschfeld's work. A prominent Nazi book burning in 1933 destroyed much of the library that Hirschfeld and his community had amassed. Hirschfeld himself then had to flee Nazi Germany as the institute was sacked. He was targeted not only for his research but also for being Jewish and gay.[3]

While trans medicine was hardly new in the post–World War II era, wartime research on hormone medications had led to a massively expanded sense of possibility. And while hormones were first clinically prescribed for non-trans people, many trans people who learned of estrogen and testosterone had begun to make their way to hospitals and clinics, hoping to transition. In the mid-1950s, a consequential new medical diagnosis was invented called "transsexuality." But the transsexual was also a new kind of cultural figure, not just a medical diagnosis. While trans people's history stretches back much farther (see part I of this book), in 1952 the entire world was introduced to a transsexual woman named Christine Jorgensen.

Jorgensen's story of transition, which made global headlines, was sensational because she seemed to embody something of the spirit of the 1950s. Having served as a soldier in the war, Jorgensen, after her transition from a conventional white man to a "blonde bombshell," was irresistible for the press invested in American empire and global cultural influence. Yet Jorgensen had actually been forced to travel to Denmark for surgery because it was nearly impossible to access in the United States. When she returned to New York City, her story had already been leaked to the press, which swarmed a glamorous and charming Jorgensen on the tarmac at the airport. She became an instant celebrity, and her American doctor, the endocrinologist Harry Benjamin, introduced the transsexual medical model to the world along with her, while also fielding thousands of letters from trans people who wrote to them for help finding health care.[4]

The transsexual medical model was deeply flawed from the outset and introduced many of the bizarre structures and extreme harms that continue to affect trans people in health care to this day. Benjamin was disappointed that he could find no explanation for why people who seemed, by scientific standards, to be biologically and psychologically "normal" wanted nevertheless to transition and change their bodies to match who they knew themselves to be. Trans people had often been lumped in with gay people—then diagnosed as homosexual—as dangerous degenerates and criminals, subject to a long history of police harassment and imprisonment. Cross-dressing was still illegal in most places in the United States, where it was criminal merely to walking down the street wearing clothing of another gender. In short, it had been exceptionally difficult for doctors who were willing to help trans people to succeed in getting them access to surgery.

Elmer Belt, a plastic surgeon in Los Angeles who agreed in the 1950s to perform gender-affirming surgeries for both trans women and men, was frustrated to find that local hospital boards would almost always cancel his procedures, citing vague concerns about legality.[5] Belt and Benjamin felt they needed to make transsexual medicine as respectable as possible so as to crack open the door to practicing the specialty in the United States, or else only Christine Jorgensen and a select few like her would ever succeed in accessing surgery. Their solution, however, was extremely conservative. Belt and Benjamin were part of a generation of clinicians who invented what is called the gatekeeping model of trans medicine.

The gatekeeping model refers to a system designed, on purpose, to *exclude* most people from health care. Strangely, then, trans medicine was invented as a subfield in order to *restrict* as much as possible access to gender transition, rather than make it a widespread possibility. This contradictory rationale was based in a profound dehumanization of trans people as unhappy victims in need of medical rescue. Writing in a medical journal in 1967, Benjamin claimed that "untreated transsexuals are among the most miserable people I have ever met." He contended that their "extreme unhappiness" in having the wrong body "brings them to the verge of suicide or self-mutilation."[6] The advantage of this high-stakes narrative was that it allowed Benjamin to present hormones and surgery as lifesaving treatment. In other words, Benjamin tried to override the prejudices of his colleagues in the medical profession by confirming their view and construing trans people as mentally ill. If psychotherapy and conversion therapy all had failed to force trans people to give up living trans lives, then trans medicine could claim to be acting out of compassion by granting them access to hormones and surgery. If the mind could not be forcibly converted, then the body would be reluctantly adjusted by endocrinologists and surgeons.

To coerce trans people to comply with this extremely conservative and disparaging narrative, the first generation of "gender clinics" that opened around the United States in the 1960s adopted stringently narrow criteria of eligibility.[7] Only people who swore they were heterosexual, wished to pass after surgery, and would then disappear into normal society could be admitted as patients. The first gender clinic to offer surgery in the United States, at Johns Hopkins Hospital, created the requirement of "the real life test," whereby anyone who wanted surgery would first have to risk living as a visibly trans person in society for a year as a precondition. Trans people's exposure to discrimination, harassment, and violence during that period when health care was being explicitly denied them was meant to confirm their deservingness. When Stanford University opened a gender clinic in 1968, the test was expanded to two years. Anyone who did not couch their request for transition in life-or-death terms, or anyone who strayed from the norm of American gender conformity, would be rejected. As a result, few trans people were able to get a transsexual diagnosis. Most had to approximate the ideal of Christine Jorgensen in some way: white, middle class, heterosexual, and wanting nothing more than to be utterly conventional. Lou Sullivan, one of the first American advocates for gay trans men, was famously turned away from Stanford because he was gay.[8]

The architects of the gatekeeping model claimed that they had devised a way to determine who was "really" transsexual and could therefore ensure that no one was accessing hormones and surgery who might later regret the decision. We continue to hear echoes of this anxiety today, more often in relation to teenagers who want to transition. But, in reality, historians have found that clinicians like Benjamin and Belt were far more preoccupied with their reputations than with science when they created this system for mitigating the risk of regretting transition. They were in fact mostly worried that disgruntled patients might sue them for delivering poor surgical outcomes. The outrageously restrictive diagnostic criteria for determining who was truly transsexual was about medical diagnosis only on the surface and was mostly a way to avoid lawsuits. By granting transition only to those patients who could pass all of their rigorous standards, they minimized the chance of any trans people contesting their work or pushing back on their authority in general.[9]

As a result, merely a tiny fraction of trans people were able to access transition through the gender clinics that sprang up around university hospitals in the 1960s, a number amounting to hundreds rather than thousands. As historian Joanne Meyerowitz found, it wasn't until the 1970s, when surgeons began opening private clinics whose only criterion was the ability to pay, that many trans people could even hope to access surgery.[10] Yet well into the twenty-first century, medical transition has remained out of reach for the vast majority of trans people because trans medicine has rarely been covered by private or public insurance. It simply costs too much money, or passing through the gate of eligibility is still too difficult. Most trans people have actually transitioned partially or entirely outside institutional medicine, which in the community is called DIY, or do-it-yourself.

The gatekeeping model has caused a litany of serious harm to trans people. And it has only recently begun to change. Today we are far more likely to encounter the phrase *gender-affirming care model*, which is the result of decades of trans advocacy and activism pushing the medical community to take responsibility for the serious damage it has inflicted by withholding hormones and surgeries from trans people that are available to non-trans people. From a historical perspective, the shift to gender-affirming care is perhaps the single largest positive change of the past century in trans health care. Gender-affirming care does precisely what it says: it converts medical providers from evaluators and gatekeepers into facilitators and supporters. Trans medicine would no longer operate by determining who "really is" trans with flimsy and unscientific criteria but would instead accept trans people's wants and needs as real and valuable.[11]

I cautiously use the conditional *would* because it is far from certain that the gender-affirming care model is being adopted uniformly. At the same time, it is precisely this less harmful model that is banned in many US states and is opposed by some health care providers for being too permissive. Even when health care institutions adopt the gender-affirming care model as a standard of care, and follow the recommendations of mainstream medical associations, the insurance system often hobbles it in practice. Even if adults are supposed to be able to enter their primary care provider's office, explain that they would like to transition, and walk out with a prescription for hormones, many insurance regulations still require a diagnosis of "gender dysphoria" according to the indicators of the *Diagnostic and Statistical Manual of Mental Disorders*, a requirement that returns the clinician to a traditional gatekeeping role. Not just providers but insurers continue to play the role of deciding which trans people are *trans enough* to receive the care that the affirmative model would offer, were it allowed to operate properly, without placing so heavy a burden of proof on those seeking care.

Ultimately, then, the present landscape of trans medicine is not just uncertain but, because it is politicized, is also deeply imperiled. Misrepresenting trans medicine in law, policy making, punditry, and moral panic further delegitimizes trans people. It is becoming extremely difficult for trans people to continue the work of critiquing and challenging the ongoing harms of medicalization when that medicalization is also being weaponized against them as a group. It is in this present-day context, when the pressure on trans people has never been higher, that the history of trans medicine bears down too. The chapters of part IV urgently open windows onto the challenges that trans health care faces in the twenty-first century as much as they remind us that the battles of the previous century for dignity, access, and affirmation have also yet to be won.

Notes

1. The WPATH Standards of Care are currently available in their seventh edition (https://www.wpath.org/publications/soc). As of this writing, the standards are being revised for the eighth edition, a highly contested and controversial process.
2. Aren Z. Aizura, *Mobile Subjects: Transnational Imaginaries of Gender Reassignment* (Durham, NC: Duke University Press, 2018).
3. Ralf Dose, *Magnus Hirschfeld: The Origins of the Gay Liberation Movement*, trans. Edward H. Willis (New York: Monthly Review Press, 2014).
4. For more on Christine Jorgensen, see Susan Stryker, *Transgender History: The Roots of Today's Revolution*, 2nd ed. (New York: Seal Press, 2017); and Joanne Meyerowitz, *How Sex Changed: A History of Transsexuality in the United States*, new ed. (Cambridge, MA: Harvard University Press, 2004).
5. Jules Gill-Peterson, *Histories of the Transgender Child* (Minneapolis: University of Minnesota Press, 2018), 137.
6. Harry Benjamin, "Transvestism and Transsexualism in the Male and Female," *Journal of Sex Research* 3, no. 2 (1967): 107–27, 110.
7. See Meyerowitz, *How Sex Changed*.
8. Lou Sullivan, *We Both Laughed in Pleasure: The Selected Diaries of Lou Sullivan* (New York: Nightboat, 2019).

9. Beans Velocci, "Standards of Care: Uncertainty and Risk in Harry Benjamin's Transsexual Classifications," TSQ: *Transgender Studies Quarterly* 8, no. 4 (2021): 462–80.
10. Meyerowitz, *How Sex Changed*.
11. Notable gender-affirming care statements of best practices are those of the American Association of Medical Colleges (2021), https://www.aamc.org/news-insights/press-releases/aamc-statement-gender-affirming-health-care-transgender-youth; the American Psychological Association (2018), https://www.apa.org/pubs/books/The-Gender-Affirmative-Model-Chapter-1-Sample.pdf; the American Psychiatric Association (2018), https://www.psychiatry.org/File%20Library/About-APA/Organization-Documents-Policies/Policies/Position-2018-Access-to-Care-for-Transgender-and-Gender-Diverse-Individuals.pdf; and the American Academy of Pediatrics (2022), https://publications.aap.org/aapnews/news/19021/AAP-continues-to-support-care-of-transgender.

Chapter 20

Sex and Gender Both Shape Your Health, in Different Ways

L. F. CARVER

WHEN YOU THINK ABOUT GENDER, what comes to mind? Is it anatomy or the way someone dresses or acts? Do you think of gender as binary: male or female? Do you think it predicts sexual orientation?

Gender is often equated with sex—by researchers as well as by those they research, especially in the health arena. I once searched a database for health-related research articles with *gender* in the title. Of the 10 articles that came up first in the list, every single one used *gender* as a synonym for sex.

Although gender can be related to sex, it is a very different concept. Gender is generally understood to be socially constructed and can differ depending on society and culture. Sex, on the other hand, is defined by chromosomes and anatomy, designated male or female. It also includes intersex people, whose bodies are not typically male or female, often with characteristics of both sexes.

Researchers often assume that all biologically female people will be more similar to one another than to those who are biologically male and so group them together in their studies. They do not consider the various sex- and gender-linked social roles and constraints that can also affect their health. This results in policies and treatment plans that are homogenous.[1]

Masculine, Cisgender, Gender Fluid, and Other Terms

The term *gender* was originally developed to describe people who did not identify with their biological sex. John Money, a pioneering gender researcher, explained, "Gender identity is your own sense or conviction of maleness or femaleness; and gender role is the cultural stereotype of what is masculine and feminine."[2]

There are now many terms used to describe gender—some of the earliest ones in use were *feminine*, *masculine*, and *androgynous* (a combination of masculine and feminine characteristics). Other terms for describing gender have come into usage more recently: *bigender* (expressing two distinct gender identities), *gender fluid* (moving between gendered behavior that is feminine and masculine depending on the situation) and *agender* or *undifferentiated* (not identifying with a particular gender or genderless). If a person's gender is consistent with their sex (e.g., a biologically female person is feminine), that person is considered *cisgender*.

Gender does not tell us about sexual orientation. For example, a woman (her sex) who is feminine (her gender) may define herself as straight or anywhere on the LGBTQIA (lesbian, gay, bisexual, transgender, queer or questioning, intersex, and asexual or allied) spectrum. The same goes for a feminine man.

Femininity Can Affect Your Heart

When gender has actually been measured in health-related research, the labels *masculine*, *feminine*, and *androgynous* have traditionally been used. Research shows that health outcomes are not homogeneous for the sexes, meaning that all biological females do not have the same vulnerabilities to illnesses and diseases nor do all biological males.

Gender is one of the things that can influence these differences. For example, when the gender of participants is considered, "higher femininity scores among men, for example, are associated with lower incidence of coronary artery disease . . . [and] female well-being may suffer when women adopt workplace behaviours traditionally seen as masculine."[3]

In another study, quality of life was better for androgynous men and women with Parkinson's disease.[4] In cardiovascular research, people who are more masculine were found to have a greater risk of cardiovascular disease than those who were more feminine.[5] And research with cancer patients found that both patients and their caregivers who were feminine or androgynous were at lower risk of depression-related symptoms as compared with those who were masculine or undifferentiated.[6]

However, as mentioned earlier, many health researchers do not measure gender, despite the existence of tools and strategies for doing so. They may try to guess gender based on sex and/or what someone looks like. But it is rare that they ask people.

A Tool for Researchers

The self-report gender measure (SR-Gender) is a simple tool that I developed and first used in a study of aging, specifically for health research.[7]

The SR-Gender asks a simple question: "Most of the time would you say you are . . . ?" The question is followed by a series of answer choices: "very feminine," "mostly feminine," "a mix of masculine and feminine," "neither masculine or feminine," "mostly masculine," "very masculine," or "other." The option to answer "other" is important and reflects the constant evolution of gender. As other genders are shared, the SR-Gender can be adapted to reflect these different categorizations. It's also important to note that the SR-Gender is not meant for in-depth gender research but rather for health and/or medical studies, where it can be used in addition to, or instead of, sex.

Using gender when describing sex just muddies the waters. Including the actual gender of research participants, as well as their sex, in health-related studies will enrich our understanding of illness. By asking people to tell us their sex and gender, health researchers may be able to understand why people experience illness and disease differently.

Notes

1. Susan P. Phillips, "Including Gender in Public Health Research," *Public Health Reports* 126, no. 3 Suppl. (2011), 16–21, https://doi.org/10.1177/00333549111260s304.
2. John Money, "The Concept of Gender Identity Disorder in Childhood and Adolescence after 39 Years," *Journal of Sex & Marital Therapy* 20, no. 3 (1994): 163–77, 163, https://doi.org/10.1080/00926239408403428.
3. Phillips, "Including Gender in Public Health Research," 126.
4. O. Moore, S. Kreitler, M. Ehrenfeld, and N. Giladi, "Quality of Life and Gender Identity in Parkinson's Disease," *Journal of Neural Transmission* 112, no. 11 (2005): 1511–22, https://doi.org/10.1007/s00702-005-0285-5.
5. Robert-Paul Juster and Sonia Lupien, "A Sex- and Gender-Based Analysis of Allostatic Load and Physical Complaints," *Gender Medicine* 9, no. 6 (2012): 511–23, https://doi.org/10.1016/j.genm.2012.10.008.
6. Vanessa I. Pikler and Chris Brown, "Cancer Patients' and Partners' Psychological Distress and Quality of Life: Influence of Gender Role," *Journal of Psychosocial Oncology* 28, no. 1 (2010): 43–60. The data set behind the study is also available: Vanessa I. Pikler and Chris Brown, "Cancer Patients' and Partners' Psychological Distress: Influence of Gender Role," *PsycEXTRA Dataset*, 2008, https://doi.org/10.1037/e489012008-001.
7. Lisa F. Carver, Rob Beamish, and Susan P. Phillips, "Successful Aging: Illness and Social Connections," *Geriatrics* 3, no. 1 (2018): 3, https://doi.org/10.3390/geriatrics3010003.

Chapter 21

I'm a Pediatrician
Who Cares for Transgender Kids—

*Here's What You Need to Know about Social Support,
Puberty Blockers, and Other Medical Options That
Improve the Lives of Transgender Youth*

MANDY COLES

WHEN CHARLIE, a 10-year-old boy, came in for his first visit, he didn't look at me or my colleague. Angry and crying, he insisted to us that he was cisgender—that he was a boy and had been born male. A few months before Charlie came into our office, he had handed a note to his mother with four simple words, "I am a boy." Up until that point Charlie had been living in the world as female—the sex he was assigned at birth—though that was not how he felt inside. Charlie was suffering from severe gender dysphoria: the sense of distress someone feels when their gender identity doesn't match up with their assigned gender.

I am a pediatrician and adolescent medicine specialist who has been caring for transgender youth for over a decade using what is called a gender-affirmative approach.[1] In this type of care, medical and mental health providers work side by side to provide education to the patient and family, guide people to social support, address mental health issues, and discuss medical interventions.

Getting on the Same Page

The first thing our team does is make sure our patients and families understand what gender care is. We always begin initial visits in the same way: "Our goal is to support you and your family on this journey, whatever that may look like for you. My name is Mandy, and I am one of the doctors at CATCH—the Child and Adolescent Transgender Center for Health program.[2] I use she/her pronouns." Sharing pronouns helps transgender people feel seen and validated.

We then ask patients and families to share their gender journey so that we can better understand where they are coming from and where they hope to go. Charlie's story is one we often hear. A kid may not think much about gender until puberty but then begins to experience worsening gender dysphoria when their body starts changing in what feels like the wrong way.

Social Transitions with Family Help

Transgender and gender-diverse youth (those whose gender identity doesn't conform to the norms expected of their

assigned sex) may face transphobia and discrimination and
then experience alarmingly higher rates of depression, anxiety, self-harm, and suicide than their cisgender peers.[3] One
option can be to socially transition to their identified gender,
both at home and in the outside world.[4]

An important first step is to help parents become allies
and advocates. Connecting parents with one-to-one as well
as group support can facilitate education and acceptance,
while helping families process their own experience. Charlie's
parents had been attending a local parent group that helped
them better understand gender dysphoria.

In addition to being accepted at home, young people
often want to live in the world in their identified gender. This
can involve changing their name and pronouns and coming
out to friends and family. It can also include using public bathrooms and participating on single-sex sports teams for their
identified gender, as well as dressing or doing other things
like binding breasts or tucking back male genitalia to present
more in line with their gender identity. Though more research
needs to be done, studies show that youth who socially transition have rates of depression similar to cisgender peers.

Many young people find that making a social transition
can be an important step in affirming their identity. For those
who still struggle with depression, anxiety, and managing
societal transphobia, seeing a therapist who has knowledge

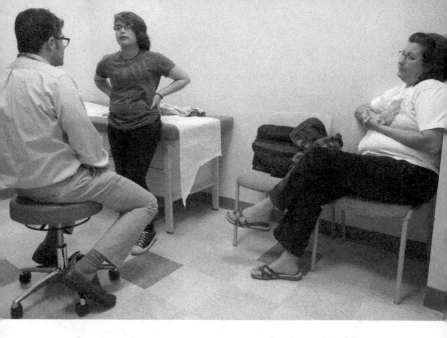

of and experience with gender-diverse identities and gender dysphoria can also be helpful.

However, most young people also need to make physical changes to their bodies as well to feel truly comfortable.

Gender-Affirming Medical Interventions

When I first met Charlie, he had already socially transitioned but was still experiencing gender dysphoria. Charlie, like many people, wanted his physical body to match his gender identity, and this can be achieved only through medical interventions—namely, puberty blockers, hormonal medications, or surgery.

For patients like Charlie who have started experiencing early female or male puberty, hormone blockers are typically the first option. These medications work like a pause button on the physical changes caused by puberty. They are well studied, safe, and completely reversible. If a person stops taking hormone blockers, their body will resume going through puberty as it would have. Blockers give people time to explore gender further and to develop social supports. Studies demonstrate that hormone blockers reduce depression, anxiety, and risk of suicide among transgender youth.

Once a person has started or completed puberty, taking prescribed hormones can help people match their bodies with their gender identities.[5] One of my patients, Zoe, is an 18-year-old transgender woman who has already completed male puberty. She is taking estrogen and a medication to block the effects of testosterone. Together, these will help Zoe's body develop breasts, reduce hair growth, and have an overall more female shape.

Leo, another one of my patients, is a 16-year-old transgender man who is using testosterone. Testosterone will deepen Leo's voice, help him grow facial hair, and lead to a more male body shape. In addition to testosterone, transgender men can use an additional short-term medication to stop menstruation. For nonbinary people like my 15-year-old patient Ty, who is not exclusively masculine or feminine, my colleagues and I personalize their treatments to meet their specific need.

The health risks from taking hormones are incredibly small—not significantly different, in fact, than the risks a cisgender person faces from the hormones in their body. Some prescribed hormone effects are partially reversible, but others are more permanent, such as deepening of the voice and growth of facial hair or breasts. Hormones can also impact fertility,[6] so I always make sure that my patients and their families understand the effects thoroughly.

The most permanent medical options available are gender-affirming surgeries. These operations can include changes to genitals, chest or breasts, and facial structure. Surgeries are not easily reversible, so my colleagues and I always make sure that patients fully understand this decision. Some people think gender-affirming surgeries go too far and that minors are too young to make such a big decision. But based on available research and my own experience, patients who get these surgeries experience improvements in their quality of life through a reduction in dysphoria.[7] I have been told by patients that gender-affirming surgery "literally saved my life. I was free [from dysphoria]."

Ongoing Gender Care

In March 2021, nearly five years after our first visit, Charlie walked into my exam room. When we first met, he was struggling with his gender, anxiety, and depression. This time, he immediately started talking about playing hockey, hanging out with friends, and making the honor roll. He had been on hormone blockers for five years and testosterone for almost a year. With the help of a supportive family and a gender-competent therapist, Charlie was thriving.

Being transgender is not something that goes away. It is something my patients live with for their entire lives. Our multidisciplinary care team continues to see patients like Charlie on a regular basis, often following them into young adulthood. While more research is always needed, a gender-affirmative approach and evidence-based medicine allow young transgender people to live in the world as their authentic selves. This improves quality of life and saves lives, as one of our transgender patients said about his experience receiving gender-affirming care: "I honestly don't think I would be here had I not been allowed to transition at that point. I'm not always 100 percent. But I have hope. I am happy to see tomorrow, and I know I will achieve my dreams."

Notes

1. Marco A. Hidalgo, Diane Ehrensaft, Amy C. Tishelman, Leslie F. Clark, Robert Garofalo, Stephen M. Rosenthal, Norman P. Spack, and Johanna Olson, "The Gender Affirmative Model: What We Know and What We Aim to Learn," *Human Development* 56, no. 5 (2013): 285–90, https://doi.org/10.1159/000355235.
2. "CATCH—Child and Adolescent Transgender Center for Health," Boston Medical Center, n.d., https://www.bmc.org/transgender-child-adolescent-center.
3. Johanna Olson, Sheree M. Schrager, Marvin Belzer, Lisa K. Simons, and Leslie F. Clark, "Baseline Physiologic and Psychosocial Characteristics of Transgender Youth Seeking Care for Gender Dysphoria," *Journal of Adolescent Health* 57, no. 4 (2015): 374–80, https://doi.org/10.1016/j.jadohealth.2015.04.027.
4. Michelle Marie Johns, Oscar Beltran, Heather L. Armstrong, Paula E. Jayne, and Lisa C. Barrios, "Protective Factors among Transgender and Gender Variant Youth: A Systematic Review by Socioecological Level," *Journal of Primary Prevention* 39, no. 3 (2018): 263–301, https://doi.org/10.1007/s10935-018-0508-9.
5. Annelou L. C. de Vries, Jenifer K. McGuire, Thomas D. Steensma, Eva C. F. Wagenaar, Theo A. H. Doreleijers, and Peggy T. Cohen-Kettenis, "Young Adult Psychological Outcome after Puberty Suppression and Gender Reassignment," *Pediatrics* 134, no. 4 (2014): 696–704, https://doi.org/10.1542/peds.2013-2958.
6. Shira Baram, Samantha A. Myers, Samantha Yee, and Clifford L. Librach, "Fertility Preservation for Transgender Adolescents and Young Adults: A Systematic Review," *Human Reproduction Update* 25, no. 6 (2019): 694–716, https://doi.org/10.1093/humupd/dmz026.
7. Johanna Olson-Kennedy, Jonathan Warus, Vivian Okonta, Marvin Belzer, and Leslie F. Clark, "Chest Reconstruction and Chest Dysphoria in Transmasculine Minors and Young Adults," *JAMA Pediatrics* 172, no. 5 (2018): 431–36, https://doi.org/10.1001/jamapediatrics.2017.5440.

Chapter 22

Two Classes of Trans Kids Are Emerging—
Those Who Have Access to Puberty Blockers and Those Who Don't

TRAVERS

FOR PEOPLE who have never thought about it before, it might sound reasonable to require trans kids to wait until they're adults before they can receive certain forms of care known as gender-affirming treatment. But this actually prevents kids from accessing treatment before and during a crucial period of development: puberty.

When I was researching my book *The Trans Generation: How Trans Kids and Their Parents Are Creating a Gender*

Revolution, I observed how not all trans kids can access the care they want or need during this critical stage of life. This unequal access to gender-affirming health care, which occurs across state lines and socioeconomic divides, could cause two "classes" of transgender people in the United States to emerge: those who are able to take hormone blockers and those who aren't able to do so. Those in the latter group can endure more financial hardship, physical pain, and mental anguish later in life, while becoming much more vulnerable to discrimination and violence.

A Paradigm Shift in Trans Treatment

For decades, many kids who didn't conform to the gender expected of them were forced to endure treatments designed to "cure" their gender nonconformity. This form of therapy, called "reparative" or "corrective," typically involved instructing parents—and sometimes teachers—to subject children to constant surveillance and correction. If a child acted in ways that didn't align with gender-expected behaviors, psychologists told caregivers to withhold affection and mete out punishments.

For example, in the 1970s, a boy with the pseudonym Kraig was a patient at UCLA's "feminine boy project," a government-funded experiment that sought to evaluate ways to reverse feminine behavior in boys. Kraig was subjected to shame-inducing treatments, with therapists counseling his father to beat Kraig when he failed to conform to masculine norms.[1]

He ended up committing suicide as an adult.

In recent years, however, there has been what transgender studies scholar Jake Pyne has called "a paradigm shift" in treatment.[2] An ever-expanding body of research shows that family support, social acceptance, and access to supportive health care produce the best outcomes for transgender kids.[3]

In 2011, the World Professional Association for Transgender Health took a position against gender-reparative therapy, stating that any therapy that seeks to change the gender identity of a patient is unethical. Changes to the law have followed suit. For example, in 2014, California passed the Student Success and Opportunity Act to ban reparative therapy and require that schools permit transgender children to participate in activities and to access spaces and facilities according to their self-determined gender categories.

Buying Time

As corrective or reparative programs have lost legitimacy, publicly and privately funded gender clinics featuring affirming models of treatment for trans kids have sprung up across the United States. Affirming treatment focuses on enabling kids' families to embrace their child's gender identity and supporting them in dealing with any resulting discrimination or mental health issues. This treatment model doesn't steer patients toward any particular gender identity. However, if a child makes the decision to transition to another gender, a number of medical interventions are available.

According to the clinical literature on gender-affirming practice, the first goal of medical treatment is to buy time for kids.[4] This is done through puberty-suppression therapy, via hormone blockers. The thinking goes that by delaying the onset of puberty, gender-nonconforming kids won't be rushed into a decision before they experience the irreversible

development of secondary sex characteristics. The second goal is for kids to have a more "normal" and satisfactory appearance as adults. To accomplish both goals, access to hormone blockers is crucial.

For example, most children who have been assigned female at birth and take hormone blockers will not need top surgery. Meanwhile, children who have been assigned male at birth and take hormone blockers won't later need to mitigate or reverse characteristics spurred by puberty: a deeper voice, facial hair, a visible Adam's apple, and other results of male puberty that cannot be reversed. Having the opportunity to take hormone blockers has been linked to reduced mental health vulnerability in transgender adults.[5]

What's more, children who are taking hormone blockers can decide to stop doing so at any time. They will then go through puberty in accord with their assigned sex at birth.

Four friends who are transitioning from
male to female hang out together.
Adam Gray/Barcroft Media via Getty Images

A Divide Emerges

Transitioning is possible after going through puberty, but it's much more difficult for trans people to look the way they want to look. It's also a lot more expensive.

This is where the divide opens up. Not everyone has supportive parents, good health insurance, and doctors who are able to provide puberty-suppression therapy. Nor does everyone live in a state with progressive legislation. When conducting research for my book, I found that access was a big theme to emerge.

At the age of 16, Nathan, for example, hated his post-pubescent body so much that he engaged in self-harm. (The names used in my book are pseudonyms, as required by research protocol.) The top surgery he so desperately needed was out of reach because his family simply couldn't afford it. His mom, Nora, described being terrified that Nathan would kill himself because of this lack of access. "It's all because of this damn top surgery," she told me. "And I am literally terrified, because I know for a fact that once he gets this done, he's going to be a totally different child. And it kills me that I can't do anything."

Seven-year-old Esme, on the other hand, had a different experience. She knew clearly from a young age that male puberty was not what she wanted and was able to communicate this to her parents. And because of her parents' support and access to affirming health care, she told me that she's planning to take hormone blockers when she's old enough. Later, she'll take cross-sex hormones, which will result in the development of secondary sex characteristics consistent with her self-defined gender identity. Whether Esme chooses to be openly transgender as an adult will be mostly up to her; her physical appearance won't mark her as trans.

Then there are the ways poverty and race are intertwined. Because Black, Native American, and Latino trans kids are disproportionately likely to be living in poverty, they're less likely to have access to crucial treatments at a young age that will make it easier to be a transgender adult.[6]

And trans kids who are nonbinary—meaning they don't feel like they're strictly male or female—also face challenges in accessing affirming health care. Many medical professionals continue to see trans health care within a binary model: patients are transitioning to either male or female. Stef, who's 14 years old and nonbinary, told me they had a far easier time accessing puberty blockers when they were asserting that they were a girl than when they subsequently adopted a nonbinary identity.

A Matter of Life or Death

Ultimately, these disparities in access have repercussions. For example, research indicates a significant improvement in quality of life among adult transgender women who have undergone facial feminization surgery, which involves surgically altering facial bones and soft tissue to conform with female gender norms. However, this is an expensive and painful procedure that transgender girls can forgo simply by having puberty-suppression treatment.

Of course, some trans people don't understand themselves to be trans early enough to advocate for themselves. And that's OK. But the majority of transgender children remain invisible—unable to articulate their feelings and longings because of unwelcoming and unsupportive environments.

Now, though, the availability of gender-affirming health care for teens is under threat in ways that go beyond insurance, cost, and familial support. In states that lack this availability, it's a societal rejection of treatment that is, for some trans teens, a matter of life or death.

Notes

1. George A. Rekers and O. Ivar Lovaas, "Behavioral Treatment of Deviant Sex-Role Behaviors in a Male Child," *Journal of Applied Behavior Analysis* 7, no. 2 (1974): 173–90, https://doi.org/10.1901/jaba.1974.7-173.
2. Jake Pyne, "Gender Independent Kids: A Paradigm Shift in Approaches to Gender Non-conforming Children," *Canadian Journal of Human Sexuality* 23, no. 1 (2014): 1–8, https://doi.org/10.3138/cjhs.23.1.co1.
3. Edgardo Menvielle, "A Comprehensive Program for Children with Gender Variant Behaviors and Gender Identity Disorders," *Journal of Homosexuality* 59, no. 3 (2012): 357–68, https://doi.org/10.1080/00918369.2012.653305.
4. S. Giordano, "Lives in a Chiaroscuro. Should We Suspend the Puberty of Children with Gender Identity Disorder?," *Journal of Medical Ethics* 34, no. 8 (2008): 580–84, https://doi.org/10.1136/jme.2007.021097.
5. Tiffiny A. Ainsworth and Jeffrey H. Spiegel, "Quality of Life of Individuals with and without Facial Feminization Surgery or Gender Reassignment Surgery," *Quality of Life Research* 19, no. 7 (2010): 1019–24. https://doi.org/10.1007/s11136-010-9668-7.
6. Jules Gill-Peterson, "The Technical Capacities of the Body: Assembling Race, Technology, and Transgender," *TSQ: Transgender Studies Quarterly* 1, no. 3 (2014): 402–18, https://doi.org/10.1215/23289252-2685660.

Chapter 23

Doctors Treating Trans Youth Grapple with Uncertainty, Lack of Training

stef m. shuster

IN APRIL 2021, the Arkansas Senate passed legislation prohibiting medical providers from offering gender-affirming hormones or surgeries to trans youth. If you were to read the bill, known as the Save Adolescents from Experimentation Act, you might think the law was protecting children from physicians like Josef Mengele, the Nazi doctor who experimented on Jewish people.

"It is of grave concern to the General Assembly," the text reads, that trans youth are being allowed "to be subjects of irreversible and drastic" treatments "despite the lack of studies showing that the benefits of such extreme interventions outweigh the risks." This language is at odds with the growing evidence that blocking people from accessing gender-affirming care creates increased risks for social isolation, suicidal ideation, and depression.[1] Withholding puberty blockers from trans and nonbinary youth has also been found to negatively affect mental health.[2]

However, the hyperbolic language and imagery of brutal experimentation prevents medical providers from honestly confronting the various issues that do exist in the field of trans medicine. The punitive nature of the legislation—through which doctors can lose their licenses—further thwarts these efforts.

As I discuss in my book *Trans Medicine*, little scientific evidence exists to support the use of current trans medical treatments, therapy, or decision-making that meets evidence-based standards. Randomized controlled trials have yet to be conducted. For this reason, providers often have trepidation about working with trans people, even if they recognize that it's in the best interests of their patients to do so.

A History of Resistance

Pointing out the lack of evidence in this medical field is nothing new.[3] Providers of trans medicine have dealt with accusations of engaging in unnecessary—even immoral—experimentation and "quackery" since the mid-20th century. Many of these charges came from other doctors.

For example, in a letter to a colleague, Harry Benjamin, a well-known endocrinologist who worked during the 1950s, wrote, "I can't tell you how many of my fellows have called me aside for a heart-to-heart talk on this business of working with transsexuals. They worried about the gossip surrounding me and my office as a result of this type of work." As Benjamin suggested—and as the historical record reflects[4]—scandal overwhelmed those providers willing to offer hormone therapy for trans people. After all, an individual who requested to change their gender presentation was understood to have a mental illness, best addressed by long-term therapy.

The medical establishment has typically responded to such charges of quackery, even from other doctors,[5] by touting their specialized training, credentials, and skills in dealing with disease and illness. But for over 70 years, physicians and therapists who work with trans clients, young and old, have nonetheless been haunted by a very basic question: How might someone who is trained to manage illness and disease "treat" someone's gender identity, which is neither an illness nor a disease?

Swimming in Doubt

The question seems simple. But it reflects the ambivalence many doctors and therapists have toward trying to apply standard medical or therapeutic models to gender identities.

Take Margaret, a family care physician who had been working for about five years in trans medicine before we met one afternoon to discuss her experiences. (The names used in my research are pseudonyms.)

"I don't always know if I am doing the right thing when I work with trans patients," she told me. "I haven't been trained in this area. So, if I have a patient who has high cholesterol or is a smoker, but wants to start estrogen, what do I do? To not offer estrogen seems harmful because that would help her be able to express her gender that reflects who she is. But what about the health risks? What am I supposed to do?" (There is mixed evidence on the relationship between taking hormones and heightened risks for heart attacks or strokes.) Health care experts are used to feeling like they have a good foundation of knowledge to make informed decisions, so this can be an uneasy space for doctors like Margaret to work in.

Her experiences are not unique. After I spent time searching in the Kinsey Institute's archives, which house correspondence from mid-20th-century providers, interviewing physicians and therapists across the United States who work with trans youth and adults, and observing them at health conferences, it became clear to me that the uncertainty Margaret expressed permeates trans medicine.

Alexis, a social worker I interviewed, told me that one of the difficulties in working with trans people is that each person is unique: "There is this person and this person and this person," she explained. Trying to apply a standard model for decision-making onto trans experience is difficult. Trans people have complex ways of understanding their identities. The reason to pursue medical interventions varies from one person to the next.

Not all providers comfortably lean on this flexibility in delivering gender-affirming care or therapy. Speaking before her colleagues at a health care conference, one physician urged them to remember, before starting their patients on hormones, that "what you are looking to get at is to make sure their gender identity is clear and there are no red flags."

But there are no medical tests to confirm a trans identity. And "red flags" aren't defined or delineated in any literature or clinical guidelines.

Barriers to Understanding

Once doctors have decided to pursue a course of treatment, the science isn't exactly settled. Part of that has to do with the fact that randomized controlled trials have been implausible, given that only 0.6 percent of the population identifies as trans or nonbinary.[6]

And physicians like Margaret might feel unqualified because most providers encounter only a single "diversity" day during medical residency programs. This day covers lesbian, gay, bisexual, and transgender health care—and, in the process, conflates sexuality and gender.

Furthermore, there are few opportunities for providers to gain formal training in trans medicine or therapy. Clinical guidelines, or cookbooks for medical decision-making, for trans medicine offer providers direction about which steps to take to initiate hormone therapy or surgical interventions. But they rarely discuss how to work with trans and nonbinary people in gender-affirming ways or how to avoid creating roadblocks for trans people trying to access care.

Still, important advances have been made.

There is a small, but growing, number of studies published on the efficacy of surgical techniques or the effects of hormone therapy. The providers I interviewed acknowledged that these studies had helped them assess how much of a hormone to prescribe. But these data did little to help providers decide when to initiate, continue, or block access to hormones—or how to interact with trans and nonbinary patients in a supportive and inclusive way.

Support—Not Punishment—Needed

The providers I spoke with insisted that they're trying to do the best they can. But because of the lack of evidence and clinical experience, providers of trans medicine often depend on gut instinct to help them navigate through the murkiness of this medical field. This can lead to bias seeping into clinical encounters.[7] Providers of trans medicine may not intentionally be prejudiced against certain trans and nonbinary people. But as I point out in my book, when they rely on gut instinct, classism, racism, and homophobia can subtly influence their health care decisions.

Trans people who identify as women or men, rather than nonbinary, have an easier time accessing gender-affirming care. The clinical experience of providers has, until recently, emphasized only people transitioning from woman to man or man to woman.

Trans medicine is not exceptional in that providers work their way toward offering gender-affirming care as they must operate in other areas of medicine that are new to them. The COVID-19 pandemic has shown the difficulty that medicine has in responding to widespread uncertainty.

There are viable solutions to the concerns raised by Arkansas legislators. What if, instead of outright barring providers from offering gender-affirming care, more public funding was provided to support longitudinal studies of trans medicine? What if more opportunities were given to providers to gain formal training? This, in my view, would go a long way toward alleviating the unease that providers experience over the state of evidence in this medical field.

Notes

1. Jaclyn M. White Hughto and Sari L. Reisner, "A Systematic Review of the Effects of Hormone Therapy on Psychological Functioning and Quality of Life in Transgender Individuals," *Transgender Health* 1, no. 1 (2016): 21–31, https://doi.org/10.1089/trgh.2015.0008.

2. Jack L. Turban, Dana King, Jeremi M. Carswell, and Alex S. Keuroghlian, "Pubertal Suppression for Transgender Youth and Risk of Suicidal Ideation," *Pediatrics* 145, no. 2 (2020): e20191725, https://doi.org/10.1542/peds.2019-1725.

3. Johanna Olson-Kennedy, Yee-Ming Chan, Stephen Rosenthal, Marco A. Hidalgo, Diane Chen, Leslie Clark, Diane Ehrensaft, Amy Tishelman, and Robert Garofalo, "Creating the Trans Youth Research Network: A Collaborative Research Endeavor," *Transgender Health* 4, no. 1 (2019): 304–12, https://doi.org/10.1089/trgh.2019.0024.

4. Susan Stryker, *Transgender History: The Roots of Today's Revolution*, 2nd ed. (New York: Seal Press, 2017).

5. Paul Starr, *The Social Transformation of American Medicine: The Rise of a Sovereign Profession and the Making of a Vast Industry*. (New York: Basic Books, 1982).

6. Esther L. Meerwijk and Jae M. Sevelius, "Transgender Population Size in the United States: A Meta-regression of Population-Based Probability Samples," *American Journal of Public Health*, 107, no. 2 (2017): e1–e8, https://doi.org/10.2105/ajph.2016.303578a.

7. stef m. shuster, "Performing Informed Consent in Transgender Medicine," *Social Science & Medicine* 226 (2019): 190–97, https://doi.org/10.1016/j.socscimed.2019.02.053.

Chapter 24

Conversion Therapy Is Discredited and Increases Risk of Suicide

DONNA SHEPERIS and CARL SHEPERIS

CONVERSION THERAPY has been routinely discredited by health and mental health professions but is regularly a subject of discussion among lawmakers. Conversion therapy, which is the practice of trying to change someone's sexual orientation or gender identity, is banned in some states but not all. Why is this concerning?

Conversion therapy is linked to suicidal intent and action for LGBTQ+ individuals. When forced to engage in this therapy, LGBTQ+ youth experience higher levels of depression and lower levels of self-esteem than their counterparts who are not subject to conversion therapy.

As experts in mental health counseling, we welcome legislation that helps protect citizens from dangerous practices. But we remain concerned that, at present, many LGBTQ+ youth live in states that have no ban in place protecting them from conversion therapy—a "treatment" that the scientific community has long since shunned.

What Is Conversion Therapy?

Conversion therapy has also been known as reparative therapy or "the gay cure." It began being practiced in the early twentieth century and is based on an outdated and incorrect notion that such identities are a choice that can be changed.

Early conversion therapy included lobotomies—surgical procedures on the brain—and aversion therapies, such as giving people electric shocks while they looked at homoerotic material. It now involves more behavioral techniques, such as forcing people to be celibate or making them dress in accordance with their assigned gender roles. It is often accompanied with requiring the person to pray and having others pray for them to make this change.

Over the past 20 years, multiple professional bodies including the American Medical Association, the American Psychological Association, and the American Counseling Association have denounced conversion therapy and determined it to be deliberately harmful and abusive to clients who are subjected to it. A 2020 study from the UCLA School of Law's Williams Institute found that gay, lesbian, and bisexual people who experienced conversion therapy were almost twice as likely to have suicidal thoughts and to have attempted suicide.[1]

These findings confirm a 2019 survey by crisis support organization the Trevor Project on LGBTQ youth mental health, which found a considerable difference in the rates of attempted suicide between respondents who were not coerced into trying to change their sexual orientation or gender identity and those who underwent conversion therapy.[2] Even more alarming, over half of transgender and nonbinary youths exposed to conversion therapy reported that they had attempted suicide in the 12 months before the survey. In addition, lack of family acceptance—commonly associated with conversion therapy—results in increased rates of substance abuse in LGBTQ individuals and declines in general health.[3]

Where Is It Legal?

Despite professionals' near-universal opposition to conversion therapy, the practice continues in the United States, particularly in Christian communities. Faith-based practices provided by pastors or lay counselors do not fall under the auspices of professional bodies that have prohibited their members from engaging in conversion therapy.

In the absence of a federal ban, cities and states have taken it upon themselves to protect young LGBTQ Americans. As of January 2022, conversion therapy was banned in fewer than half of the states in the United States. The first state to ban the practice was New Jersey in 2013. In addition to the states with outright bans, three states—Alabama, Florida, and Georgia—have passed legislation banning conversion therapy, but federal circuit court injunctions in place prevent the enforcement of the states' prohibitions.

The partial lack of state bans leaves around half of

America's adult LGBTQ population living in states and cities where conversion therapy is currently legal, according to the independent think tank Movement Advancement Project. The Southern Poverty Law Center estimates that there are almost 200 intensive conversion therapy programs for families and teens in these states.

The Legal Loophole

In these state lacking bans, "silent" states as we call them, a legal loophole exists: although professional bodies ban their members from conducting conversion therapy, some practitioners with no relevant degree, certification, or license nevertheless practice conversion therapy by operating outside professional associations.[4] Many of them cite religious reasons for engaging in the practice. Some even believe it unethical not to offer conversion therapy as a choice.

Bans therefore can do only so much and may not be present in the states where they are most needed. A US map shows that most states lacking any law or policy banning conversion therapy are in traditionally Republican-leaning regions in the center of the country, while states restricting or banning the practice of conversion therapy are primarily in the Northeast or on the West Coast—places that tend to lean Democratic.[5] In addition, the nine most religious states in the United States, including Alabama, Mississippi, and Tennessee, have no enforceable laws prohibiting conversion therapy. Individuals or families living in states with a ban can, of course, drive or be driven to another state without a ban in search of a place offering conversion therapy.

States that have enacted bans have often done so in the face of legal challenges. Much of the opposition has come from fundamentalist Christian groups like Focus on the Family and the American Family Association, organizations that guide individuals and families toward conversion therapy. Under the belief that same-sex attraction may occur but does not need to be acted on, many Christian organizations promote an understanding of biblical principles that condemns any sexuality outside binary, heterosexual relationships. Besides bringing legal challenges to any proposed ban, these groups provide literature supporting conversion therapy and curricula for churches to use in providing such services.

Under the Trump administration, some bans were struck down. There is a concern now among LGBTQ rights advocates that challenges to rulings that overturned bans could eventually advance a case to a conservative Supreme Court, which has tended to rule in favor of religious liberties.

A Full Ban Unlikely

Even if a federal ban on the practice were to be established—or if all US states enacted their own bans—there would still remain the potential for religious exemptions or exemptions for nonprofessionals to continue carrying out conversion therapy. A full ban on conversion therapy would require a prohibition of the practice for all: professionals, paraprofessionals, religious institutions, and laypeople. But given the ongoing legal battles over the discredited practice, it is unlikely that the United States will witness an across-the-board ban anytime soon.

Notes

1. John R. Blosnich, Emmett R. Henderson, Robert W. S. Coulter, Jeremy T. Goldbach, and Ilan H. Meyer, "Sexual Orientation Change Efforts, Adverse Childhood Experiences, and Suicide Ideation and Attempt among Sexual Minority Adults, United States, 2016–2018," *American Journal of Public Health* 110, no. 7 (2020): 1024–30, https://doi.org/10.2105/ajph.2020 .305637. "LGB People Who Have Undergone Conversion Therapy Almost Twice as Likely to Attempt Suicide," Williams Institute, UCLA School of Law, June 24, 2020, https://williamsinstitute.law.ucla.edu/press/lgb -suicide-ct-press-release/.
2. Trevor Project, *National Survey on LGBTQ Mental Health,* section "Conversion Therapy & Change Attempts," 2019, https://www .thetrevorproject.org/survey-2019/?section=Conversion-Therapy-Change -Attempts.
3. Wansong Harley, "The Constitutionality of Conversion Therapy Bans," Santa Barbara and Ventura Colleges of Law, May 27, 2020, https:// www.collegesoflaw.edu/blog/2020/05/27/the-constitutionality-of -conversion-therapy-bans/.
4. Harley, "Constitutionality of Conversion Therapy Bans."
5. "Equality Maps," "Conversion 'Therapy' Laws," Movement Advancement Project, n.d., https://www.lgbtmap.org/equality-maps/conversion _therapy.

Chapter 25

Not Everyone Is Male or Female— the Growing Controversy over Sex Designation

CARL STREED JR. and FRANCES GRIMSTAD

CHECK OUT YOUR BIRTH CERTIFICATE, and you are sure to see a designation for sex. When you were born, a doctor or clinician assigned you the "male" or "female" label based on a look at your genitalia. In the United States, this has been standard practice for more than a century.[1]

But sex designation is not as simple as a glance and then a check in one box or the other. Instead, the overwhelming evidence shows that sex is not binary.[2] To put it another way, the terms *male* and *female* don't fully capture the complex biological, anatomical, and chromosomal variations that occur in the human body. That's why calls are growing to remove sex designation from birth certificates, including a 2021 recommendation from the American Medical Association.

I (Streed) am a professor of medicine who has worked extensively on lesbian, gay, bisexual, transgender, queer, intersex, and asexual (LGBTQIA+) issues. My coauthor is a professor of gynecology who is deeply involved in the health of people who are trans and intersex. Our research and clinical experience show that sex designation is not something to take for granted. For those who don't fit neatly into one of two categories, and there are millions who don't,[3] an inappropriate classification on a birth certificate can have consequences that last a lifetime.

The Problems with Sex Designation

Variations in genital anatomy happen more frequently than you might think; they occur in 0.1 to 0.2 percent of births annually.[4] In the United States, that's about 4,000 to 8,000 babies each year. Doctors examining the reproductive organs find people born with both a vagina and testes and also those born without any gonads.

And when evaluating an individual's estrogen and testosterone hormone levels, long defined as key determinants of female and male bodies, doctors find some people with vaginas who still produce significant amounts of testosterone. Because of this, testosterone is not a great indicator for defining sex; higher amounts of testosterone do not necessarily make someone male.

Even karyotyping—a laboratory procedure used since the 1950s to evaluate an individual's number and type of chromosomes—doesn't tell the whole story. While we typically expect people to have either an XX or XY pair of sex chromosomes, many people have variations that do not fit either category. These include Turner syndrome, in which a person is born with a single X chromosome, and Klinefelter syndrome, which occurs when a person is born with a combination of XXY chromosomes.

In short, human diversity has demonstrated that the binary categories of male and female are incomplete and inaccurate. Sex designation, rather than "two sizes fit all," is on a spectrum.[5] Up to 1.7 percent of the US population—more than five million Americans—have an anatomy and physiology that present intersex traits.

Binary Designations Can Be Damaging

Those with intersex traits who are assigned at birth to be female or male can experience medical care that harms them, both physically and psychologically. Sometimes physicians perform surgeries to align bodies with one of the binary categories. For example, those born with a larger than typical clitoris may have it reduced in size. But some who have had this childhood surgery suffer as adults from pain and difficulty in having sex.

Additionally, governments sometimes limit those with intersex traits from fully participating in society. For instance, in Australia, marriages have been annulled because governments have previously ruled that an intersex person—someone not seen to be 100 percent man or 100 percent woman—cannot be legally married.

Private entities often do the same. The International Olympic Committee uses cutoffs of hormone levels to determine who can compete in women's sports. As a result, some athletes have been barred from participation.

State governments have begun to acknowledge sex diversity. Some let gender-diverse people change their designation on birth certificates, although there are restrictions. Medicine too is changing. For example, some pediatric centers have stopped performing surgeries on newborns with differences in sexual development. Still, society at large has been much slower to move beyond the application of strictly binary categories.

As clinicians, we strive to be accurate. The evidence shows that using male and female as the only options on birth certificates is not consistent with scientific reality. Evidence shows that removing this designation will tell new parents that it's not sex assignment that's most important at birth but rather the celebration of a healthy and happy baby.

Notes

1. Vadim Shteyler, Jessica A. Clarke, and Eli Y. Adashi, "Failed Assignments—Rethinking Sex Designations on Birth Certificates," *New England Journal of Medicine* 383, no. 25 (2020): 2399–401, https://doi.org/10.1056/nejmp2025974.
2. Goran Štrkalj and Nalini Pather, "Beyond the Sex Binary: Toward the Inclusive Anatomical Sciences Education," *Anatomical Sciences Education* 14, no. 4 (2020): 513–18, https://doi.org/10.1002/ase.2002.
3. Melanie Blackless, Anthony Charuvastra, Amanda Derryck, Anne Fausto-Sterling, Karl Lauzanne, and Ellen Lee, "How Sexually Dimorphic Are We? Review and Synthesis," *American Journal of Human Biology* 12, no. 2 (2000): 151–66, https://doi.org/10.1002/(SICI)1520-6300(200003/04)12:2<151::AID-AJHB1>3.0.CO;2-F.
4. Mary García-Acero, Olga Moreno, Fernando Suárez, and Adriana Rojas, "Disorders of Sexual Development: Current Status and Progress in the Diagnostic Approach," *Current Urology* 13, no. 4 (2020): 169–78, https://doi.org/10.1159/000499274.
5. Frances Grimstad, Jessica Kremen, Carl G. Streed Jr., and Katharine B. Dalke, "The Health Care of Adults with Differences in Sex Development or Intersex Traits Is Changing: Time to Prepare Clinicians and Health Systems," *LGBT Health* 8, no. 7 (2021): 439–43, https://doi.org/10.1089/lgbt.2021.0018.

Chapter 26

Transgender and Nonbinary People Face Health Care Discrimination Every Day in the US

SHANNA K. KATTARI

Many people may experience anxiety when seeking medical treatment. They might worry about wait times, insurance coverage, or how far they must travel to access care. Transgender and nonbinary individuals have an added fear: gender-related discrimination. This can involve being outed by a name or gender mismatch on an insurance card, being denied care, or even being left to die. Growing scientific evidence shows that this population faces significant hurdles in many domains, including when seeking medical and mental health care.

Many transgender and nonbinary individuals, particularly those of color, report discrimination when seeking health care services. EMT = emergency medical technician. *The Conversation, CC BY-ND. Data from the* International Journal of Transgenderism *(2015)*

Rates of Discrimination

Transgender and nonbinary individuals are those whose gender does not align with the social expectations connected to the sex they were assigned at birth. Sex, usually assigned male or female at birth, is based on genitalia presented at birth, while gender is a complete sense of who one knows themselves to be.

It's difficult to estimate what percentage of the population is transgender or nonbinary. Gender identity is not included on the US Census or in most national or statewide data collection efforts. However, one study found that approximately 1.6 percent of US adults and 5 percent of adults younger than 30 years identified as trans or nonbinary.[1] Younger people are more likely to have one of these identities compared with older adults. Somewhere between 0.72 percent[2] and 3.8 percent[3] of high school–aged youth reported that they identify as transgender, nonbinary, or another identity besides the sex they were assigned at birth.

This population has many challenging experiences when compared with individuals who are not transgender. Some problems include employment and housing discrimination,[4] as well as higher rates of intimate partner violence.[5] Many of these experiences are connected to transphobia, or discrimination against transgender and nonbinary individuals.

Health researchers like me have been working to better

Health Care Discrimination.

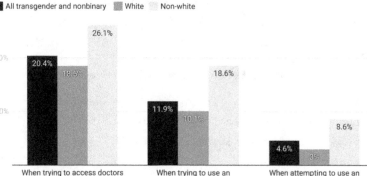

■ All transgender and nonbinary ▧ White ▨ Non-white

	When trying to access doctors or hospitals	When trying to use an emergency room	When attempting to use an ambulance or EMT
All transgender and nonbinary	20.4%	11.9%	4.6%
White	18.5%	10.1%	3%
Non-white	26.1%	18.6%	8.6%

understand the discrimination this group faces in medical settings. For example, approximately one-fifth of transgender and nonbinary individuals have been denied equal treatment when trying to access doctors or hospitals.[6]

Discrimination can come in many different forms. Medical providers might assume that all health issues are correlated with one's gender identity—for example, by assuming that pneumonia is somehow connected to hormone use or that all anxiety must be due to being transgender. Such assumptions are sometimes wryly referred to as "trans broken arm syndrome": a medical provider's attribution of any number of unrelated health issues to a trans identity. Others might be refused care or experience hurtful language or harassment.

These experiences of discrimination are exacerbated for transgender and nonbinary people of color and people with disabilities. This is true not only in medical settings but also in places like mental health centers, domestic violence centers, drug treatment programs, and rape crisis centers. In fact, those with multiple types of disabilities—whether physical, socioemotional, or learning-related—are over three times more likely to experience discrimination in all four settings as compared with nondisabled people.

Making Health Care More Inclusive

Societal stigma and bias can leave transgender and nonbinary people feeling marginalized. But there are steps that medical providers can take to promote resiliency and well-being among this population.

Transgender and nonbinary individuals have higher rates of depression and thoughts about suicide. They are also significantly more likely to attempt suicide. These increased rates are not due to being transgender but instead come from dealing with stigma, lack of acceptance, and abuse.

One study showed that, when transgender and nonbinary individuals had a primary care provider that they considered to be inclusive, they had lower rates of depression and suicidal thoughts.[7] About 54 percent of those without an inclusive provider reported current depression, compared with only 38 percent of those with such a provider.

I believe that medical and nursing schools; social work, counseling, and psychology training programs; and community organizations should make an earnest effort to better train all health care providers and social service professionals for treating trans and nonbinary people. Staff should be more comfortable treating members of this community, especially those with multiple marginalized identities, like transgender people of color. This training could include information on different language used by this community, guidance on how to use a variety of pronouns correctly, or best health care practices for working with members of this community. It could even start by simply providing a basic understanding of the difference between gender and sex. Such training could help reduce the alarming rates of discrimination faced by members of this community, as well as bolster their overall health and well-being.

Notes

1. Anna Brown, "About 5% of Young Adults in the U.S. Say Their Gender Is Different from Their Sex Assigned at Birth," Pew Research Center, June 7, 2022, https://www.pewresearch.org/fact-tank/2022/06/07/about-5 -of-young-adults-in-the-u-s-say-their-gender-is-different-from-their -sex-assigned-at-birth/.
2. Marla E. Eisenberg, Amy L. Gower, Barbara J. McMorris, Nicole Rider, Glynis Shea, Eli Coleman, "Risk and Protective Factors in the Lives of Transgender / Gender Nonconforming Adolescents," *Journal of Adolescent Health* 61, no. 4 (2017): 521–26, https://doi.org/10.1016/j .jadohealth.2017.04.014.
3. *2015 Healthy Kids Colorado Survey*, Colorado: Official State Web Portal, 2015, https://www.colorado.gov/.
4. Shanna K. Kattari, Darren L. Whitfield, N. Eugene Walls, Lisa Langenderfer- Magruder, and Daniel Ramos, "Policing Gender through Housing and Employment Discrimination: Comparison of Discrimination Experiences of Transgender and Cisgender LGBQ Individuals," *Journal of the Society for Social Work and Research* 7, no. 3 (2016): 427–47, https://doi.org /10.1086/686920.
5. Lisa Langenderfer-Magruder, Darren L. Whitfield, N. Eugene Walls, Shanna K. Kattari, Daniel Ramos, "Experiences of Intimate Partner Violence and Subsequent Police Reporting among Lesbian, Gay, Bisexual, Transgender, and Queer Adults in Colorado: Comparing Rates of Cis- gender and Transgender Victimization," *Journal of Interpersonal Violence* 31, no. 5 (2014): 855–71, https://doi.org/10.1177/0886260514556767.
6. Shanna K. Kattari and Leslie Hasche, "Differences across Age Groups in Transgender and Gender Non-conforming People's Experiences of Health Care Discrimination, Harassment, and Victimization," *Journal of Aging and Health* 28, no. 2 (2015): 285–306, https://doi.org /10.1177/0898264315590228.
7. Shanna K. Kattari, Eugene Walls, Stephanie Rachel Speer, and Leonardo Kattari, "Exploring the Relationship between Transgender-Inclusive Providers and Mental Health Outcomes among Transgender / Gender Variant People," *Social Work in Health Care* 55, no. 8 (2016): 635–50, https://doi.org/10.1080/00981389.2016.1193099.

Chapter 27

Denying Transgender Identity Has Serious Impact on Mental Health

BETHANY GRACE HOWE

"STICKS AND STONES may break my bones, but words will never hurt me," goes the playground rhyme. But the adage is only half right. According to my research on transgender mental health, words can hurt.[1]

In October 2018, the *New York Times* published a story headlined "'Transgender' Could Be Defined out of Existence under Trump Administration."[2] The story was about the Department of Health and Human Services' efforts to create a new legal definition of *sex* under Title IX, the 1972 federal civil rights law that forbids gender discrimination in education programs that get money from the government. That move would have defined sex as determined solely by the genitals that a person has at birth, strictly male or female, and unchangeable.

I study how media affects transgender identity across the United States. The travel for my work is funded in part by the Caitlyn Jenner Foundation. I maintain complete autonomy over what I research and how. From my prior research, I knew the *New York Times* story would produce negative emotions among transgender people. So I conducted an online survey of more than 100 transgender people in the 72 hours following the story's publication, to ask how negatively the story affected them on a seven-point scale. I followed this with a qualitative question about how painful those emotions were.

The proposed new definition of sex aimed to eliminate the very idea of a transgender person. Therefore, what I found was not surprising. It's one thing for people to have to defend their rights as equals in society. But when people have to defend their existence, both the frequency and degree to which transgender people experience negative emotions significantly increase.

When Words Do Damage

In my survey, more than three-quarters of respondents said they felt their identity was under increased threat. Many people noted they had already felt that way, even before the story ran. But the story had made the feelings worse. In other words, those transgender people who were already under stress became even more so.

The open-response part of the survey made clear what type of emotional impact transgender people felt after reading the story. "Shock," "horror," and "a sense of uncontrollable doom" were just some of the answers from respondents. "I feel like they're trying to erase me as a person" was a frequent response variously expressed.

For some it was more than just emotional—it took a physical toll. One transgender person told me that even though their transition had been largely free of problems, this news had left her curled up in a ball, crying on the floor of the shower.

Three people told me of a teenager they knew for whom the emotions brought on by the story were the last straw. Less than two weeks after the story was published, she tried to take her own life. Ten days after the story ran, Trans Lifeline, a national grassroots organization, reported that calls to its suicide hotline had increased by 400 percent.[3]

When Identity Is Denied

Now, can one story in a newspaper result in someone committing suicide? This would be impossible to prove. What is clear, though, is that the impact of statements or actions that are subtly and even unintentionally discriminatory, what researchers call "microaggressions," is measurable and real.[4] *Micro* is not meant to describe how the aggression is perceived but rather how effortlessly it is delivered. Research shows that microaggressions, such as being the object of a joke, the subject of a put-down—or the topic in a demeaning headline—take only take a few seconds to make their impact.[5]

A demonstrator holds a sign outside a voting center in Houston in 2015.
AP Photo / Pat Sullivan

The *New York Times* headline is an example of the specific type of microaggressions my research focuses on: those that deny transgender identity exists. The emotions these produce are intensely negative and, depending on the person, can lead to a decreased willingness to engage with others. I call this "transgender identity defense–related emotions." My previous research has examined the link between these intensely negative emotions and suicide. One in five transgender people reports having attempted suicide, a rate six times higher than that of the US population at large.

Certainly, where causation ends and correlation begins remains unknown. But there's clearly a negative impact on the mental health of transgender people when their identity is denied in this way.

Notes

1. Adrienne Shaw and D. Travers Scott, *Interventions: Communication Research and Practice* (New York: Peter Lang, 2018).
2. Erica L. Green, Katie Benner, and Robert Pear, " 'Transgender' Could Be Defined out of Existence under Trump Administration," *New York Times*, October 21, 2018, https://www.nytimes.com/2018/10/21/us/politics /transgender-trump-administration-sex-definition.html.
3. Jenni Fink, "Trans Lifeline Reportedly Receives 4 Times the Amount of Calls after Trump Memo Moves to Define Gender," *Newsweek*, October 31, 2018, https://www.newsweek.com/after-trump-admin-memo-move -define-gender-trans-lifeline-receives-4x-amount-1195253.
4. Derald Wing Sue, Christina M. Capodilupo, Gina C. Torino, Jennifer M. Bucceri, Aisha Holder, Kevin L. Nadal, and Marta Esquilin, "Racial Micro-aggressions in Everyday Life: Implications for Clinical Practice," *American Psychologist* 62, no. 4 (2007): 271–86, https://doi.org/10.1037/0003 -066X.62.4.271.
5. Michael A. Dover, "The Moment of Microaggression: The Experience of Acts of Oppression, Dehumanization, and Exploitation," *Journal of Human Behavior in the Social Environment* 26, nos. 7–8 (2016): 575–86. https://doi.org/10.1080/10911359.2016.1237920.

Part V.

Trans Rights Are Human Rights, but Rights Are Not Enough

In 2019 the United States Supreme Court issued its opinion in *Bostock v. Clayton County*. In a landmark decision, the conservative justice Neil Gorsuch, representing the majority, wrote that transgender people as a class are fully protected under federal law from discrimination in employment. The court determined that discriminating against trans people was a straightforward case of sex discrimination under existing law, deeply rooting trans civil rights in employment in a well-settled legal precedent.[1] Yet in the years since that opinion was issued, hundreds upon hundreds of pieces of state legislation have been introduced that would aim to retrench, repeal, or even ban any other potential civil right that trans people could enjoy. Just when trans civil rights were given a conservative legal grounding by the Supreme Court, trans people in some states found that they lack any other protection under the law. Many states have moved aggressively to use their administrative and policing powers to actively harass and disenfranchise trans people of all ages, pushing them out of public education, sports, health care, and basic legal personhood. How can it be that trans people's human rights are so shot through with contradiction?

As the previous parts of this book have laid out in many different arenas, gender may be a social and cultural system, but by and large it is regulated, policed, and enforced through law. The law is also one avenue through which many kinds of oppressed people, including those who are trans and nonbinary, challenge entrenched forms of discrimination. Yet it is hardly the only one. A significant body of critical trans legal scholarship has worked to explain how legal or formal equality under the law does quite little to improve the actual lives of trans and nonbinary people, especially given their disproportionate poverty.[2] While widespread legal discrimination is still the norm, including trans people in civil rights statutes does not in and of itself remedy the widespread criminalization, policing, and incarceration of poor trans people, especially Black and Latinx trans women. The continued production of curtailed life chances within the trans community in the United States is not evenly distributed but instead follows predictable fault lines of American inequality in race, class, ability, and immigration status. Even *Bostock v. Clayton County* reflects this reality.

Although the ability to contest employment discrimination is a significant legal victory, it is a hollow one to the extent that most trans people, if they have access to the formal economy at all, are likely to work poorly paid service-industry jobs. When poor trans women or trans people of color are fired from low-wage jobs due to discrimination, they are unlikely to have the financial resources needed to sue their employer under federal law. In that sense, the Supreme Court has not offered them anything tangible in interpreting the law to include them.

Part V of this book examines a number of important legal and human rights violations committed against trans people. Contributors paint a portrait of discrimination in health care, employment, housing, and family law, while also offering critical context for so-called ethical dilemmas around trans inclusion in organized sport. As the chapters show, the impulse to frame trans inclusion as an ethical dilemma is itself a way to justify and perpetuate discrimination. So often trans people's material suffering and oppression are turned into hypothetical or ethical dilemmas in order to abstract them out of reality and mischaracterize what is really at stake. For that reason, it's important to come to this final part of the book with some of the limitations of a legal or human rights perspective in mind and to know that other bodies of trans advocacy and writing are important to read alongside the contributions gathered here.

Framing trans people in conventional terms as a uniform minority population that has been hidden in the shadows, and that now deserves access to the usual trappings of Western life, is a shallow vision. Indeed, the preface and the part introductions of this book have worked to problematize that assumption and, to that effect, can be read as one long essay in six installments. In reality, there is no uniform "trans community." Trans people are an extremely diverse and divergent group of people hailing from all walks of life, not to mention countless cultures around the world that do not endorse the Western, colonial emphasis on the gender binary or even the terminology of *trans*. Significant material differences organized around race, class, national context, culture, and religion make the project of defining *trans* as any one thing a futile one. But this is not, to my mind, a problem—it is *a source of immense strength*.

Critical trans politics informed by race, class, culture, and colonialism begins to loosen the shallow demand to package groups of people in identifiable and containable minorities in need of rescue by way of benevolent recognition. By learning to listen to different trans and nonbinary people in the context of their actual lives, including the people who are excluded by trans and gender terminology because they come from different cultural and social positions, we begin to *un*learn some of the assumptions of "the trans conversation" or "the conversation around gender diversity." This project of *un*learning is in many ways just as vital as the educational import of the chapters of this book.

To move beyond a Western human rights framework, or an American civil rights framework, we might turn our attention to the legacy of the trans liberation movement that arose in the 1970s. In the aftermath of the Stonewall rebellion in New York City in 1969, when poor trans and gay people rioted and defeated the police who had raided a popular gay bar, trans activists formed new organizations under the banner of gay liberation.[3] A broad-based coalition of oppressed people affected by common problems of policing, violence, stigma, and poverty, gay and trans liberation understood itself outside the narrow terms of identity politics. The Gay Liberation Front included not just gay men and lesbians but also many trans people of different stripes who had helped lead the battle at Stonewall. But the Gay Liberation Front also reached out more broadly to ally with other movements of the day, including women's liberation, the antiwar movement, the student movement, the Black Panthers, the Puerto Rican Young Lords, and anticolonial movements around the world struggling against the reductive framing of the Cold War in terms of capitalism versus communism.[4] In the context of this broad coalition, the documents produced in the early 1970s are remarkable not just for their breadth but also for the depressing truth that not much has changed in the struggles of trans people over the past five decades. While gay and lesbian people have enjoyed the successes of de-medicalizing homosexuality, achieving unprecedented political representation, and even earning same-sex marriage rights, trans people are still demanding an end to police violence, widespread poverty, and a lack of self-determination with health care.

Here are the demands enumerated by a manifesto titled "Transvestite and Transsexual Liberation," published in a gay newspaper in 1971:

1. Abolition of all crossdressing laws and restrictions of adornment.
2. An end to exploitation and discrimination within the Gay world.
3. An end to exploitative practices of doctors and psychiatrists who work in the fields of transvestism and transsexualism. Hormone treatment and transsexual surgery should be provided for free upon demand by the state.
4. Transsexual assistance centers should be created in all cities of over one million inhabitants, under the direction of postoperative transsexuals.
5. Transvestites and transsexuals should be granted full and equal rights on all levels of society and a full voice in the struggle for the liberation of all oppressed people.
6. Transvestites who exist as members of the opposite anatomical gender should be able to obtain full identification as members of the opposite gender. Transsexuals should be able to obtain such identification commensurate to their new gender with no difficulty, and not be required to carry special identification as transsexuals. There should be no special licensing requirements of transvestites or transsexuals who work in the entertainment field.
7. Immediate release of all persons in mental hospitals or prisons, being held for transvestism or transsexualism.[5]

Of these seven demands, exactly *zero* have been achieved in the United States. Yes, cross-dressing laws are no longer on the books, yet only as recently as 2021 did New York State repeal its infamous "walking while trans" law, which was used to arrest poor trans women of color on flimsy suspicions of sex work.[6] Other countries, Nepal and India, for instance, have more substantial legal and even constitutional recognition of trans people, but, again, the gap between formal equality and material reality remains a central problem for activists and organizers.[7]

As you read part V and take away the many insights of its contributors, keep in mind the limitations of human rights: that is, Western and American models of progress that narrowly define success as assimilation to standards that have otherwise been used to dehumanize trans people. The seven demands of trans liberation, made 50 years ago, could have just as easily been made yesterday. Indeed, the children of that movement struggle on, unable and unwilling to wait for the blessing of the mainstream.

In June 2020, tens of thousands of people poured into the streets of Brooklyn dressed in all white. They gathered to rally for Black trans people, part of a momentous summer of protest and revolt in the name of Black freedom following the police murder of George Floyd in Minneapolis. The Brooklyn Liberation march was the largest march for Black trans people the planet had ever seen. And its urgency was palpable. In the span of merely 24 hours leading up to the march, another two Black trans women had been murdered: Dominique Fells in Philadelphia and Riah Milton in Ohio. In her riveting speech delivered to the crowd from the steps of the Brooklyn Museum, activist and organizer Raquel Willis announced an enduring truth to the world: "Let today be the last day that you ever doubt Black trans power."[8]

As you hold this book in your hand, and as you return to it in the future as a resource for understanding your place in the historical arc of gender in this world, hold Willis's words in your heart. Do not doubt, but embrace and give thanks for that power, one that challenges the world to prove itself good enough for *everyone* who calls it home.

Notes

1. Bostock v. Clayton County, 590 U.S. ___ (2020), Cornell Law School, https://www.law.cornell.edu/supct/pdf/17-1618.pdf.
2. Dean Spade, *Normal Life: Administrative Violence, Critical Trans Politics, and the Limits of Law* (Durham, NC: Duke University Press, 2015).
3. See Martin Duberman, *Stonewall: The Definitive Story of the LGBTQ Rights Uprising That Changed America* (New York: Plume, 2019).
4. See Hugh Ryan, "The Incredible True Adventure of Five Gay Activists in Search of the Black Panther Party," *Harper's Bazaar*, June 8, 2021, https://www.harpersbazaar.com/culture/features/a36651331/the-incredible-true-adventure-of-five-gay-activists-and-the-black-panther-party/.
5. "Transvestite and Transsexual Liberation," *Detroit Gay Liberator* 1, no. 8 (January 1, 1971): 10. Available from the *Digital Transgender Archive*, https://www.digitaltransgenderarchive.net/files/th83kz57z.
6. Jaclyn Diaz, "New York Repeals 'Walking while Trans' Law," NPR, February 3, 2021, https://www.npr.org/2021/02/03/963513022/new-york-repeals-walking-while-trans-law.
7. A. J. Agrawal, "Trans Rights in Nepal: Progress and Pitfalls," Centre for Law & Policy Research, July 6, 2020, https://clpr.org.in/blog/trans-rights-in-nepal-progress-pitfalls/.
8. Anuskha Patil, "How a March for Black Trans Lives Became a Huge Event," *New York Times*, June 15, 2020, https://www.nytimes.com/2020/06/15/nyregion/brooklyn-black-trans-parade.html.

Chapter 28

A Supreme Court Decision to Grant Protections to LGBT Workers Is an Important Interpretation of the Civil Rights Act

JULIE MANNING MAGID

NO FEDERAL LAW barring discrimination against LGBT workers in hiring, promoting, and firing existed in this country until June 2020. Although some may have believed LGBT individuals were protected from workplace discrimination following the US Supreme Court's 2015 *Obergefell v. Hodges* decision that found the fundamental right to marry to be guaranteed to same-sex couples, this was not the case.

I'm a professor of business law, and I believe the *Bostock v. Clayton County, Georgia* decision issued on June 16, 2020, could be one of the most important in the history of the Civil Rights Act.

On the Basis of Sex

Title VII of the Civil Rights Act made it illegal for employers to discriminate based on an individual's race, color, religion, sex, or national origin. In October 2019, the US Supreme Court heard three cases that raised the question of whether the act prevents discrimination against LGBT workers on the basis of sex. Two of the cases were brought by men who allegedly lost their jobs because they are gay. The third case addressed transgender discrimination in the workplace. All three cases were consolidated and decided by *Bostock v. Clayton County, Georgia.*

"On the basis of sex" are the crucial words in the Supreme Court's decision. Some commentators have expressed

surprise that two traditionally conservative justices, Chief Justice John Roberts and Justice Neil Gorsuch, joined with the four traditionally more liberal judges in the six-to-three decision.

But given the rise of *statutory originalism* and *textualism* in judicial interpretation, I don't see the result as remarkable. Originalism has it that courts should interpret laws according to their original intent or purpose. Judges who subscribe to textualism believe they should evaluate only the words of a statute enacted by Congress and not consider evidence outside the statutory language.

In this case, the clear language used by Congress in enacting Title VII determined the outcome. Justice Neil Gorsuch, who is known to employ both textualism and originalism in judicial interpretation, authored the majority opinion that extended protection from employment discrimination to millions of people.

Textualism and Originalism

Gorsuch's opinion examined "on the basis of sex" through the lenses of both textualism and originalism.

The first paragraph of the decision reads, "An employer who fires an individual for being homosexual or transgender fires that person for traits or actions it would not have questioned in members of a different sex. Sex plays a necessary and undisguisable role in the decision, exactly what Title VII

Demonstrators rallied outside the US Supreme Court in October 2019.
SAUL LOEB/AFP via Getty Images

forbids." In other words, "on the basis of sex" means "due to sex" and not, as it so often is interpreted, male or female gender.

Gorsuch goes on to write: "[The statute] tells us three times—including immediately after the words 'discriminate against'—that our focus should be on individuals, not groups." To illustrate the difference, Justice Gorsuch uses examples that relate to earlier Supreme Court Title VII cases concerning sexual stereotyping.

In 1989, the court had decided that Title VII prohibited an employer from denying opportunities to a woman based on "stereotypical notions about women's proper deportment" in *Price Waterhouse v. Hopkins*. In that case, Ann Hopkins received advice from her employer that, if she wanted to make partner at the firm, she should act more feminine.[1] The court's ruling meant that an employer couldn't penalize an employee based on gender nonconformity under Title VII.

In *Oncale v. Sundowner Offshore*[2] a unanimous Supreme Court had held that same-sex harassment is sex discrimination under Title VII. The case involved a man working on an oil rig who was bullied by other men because he was considered effeminate. That 1998 opinion was written by Justice Antonin Scalia, then the avowed originalist on the court, and opened the door for an expansion of Title VII.

Justice Gorsuch placed these cases in a textualist context when he said, "So an employer who fires a woman, Hannah, because she is insufficiently feminine and also fires a man, Bob, for being insufficiently masculine may treat men and women as groups more or less equally. But in both cases the employer fires an individual in part because of sex. Instead of avoiding Title VII exposure, this employer doubles it."

The originalist lens immediately follows in the second paragraph of the decision: "Those who adopted the Civil Rights Act might not have anticipated their work would lead to this particular result . . . But the limits of the drafters' imagination supply no reason to ignore the law's demands."

Justice Gorsuch goes on to explain why the textualist reading must prevail by noting that Title VII's protected class of sex was complicated from the start.[3] However, the original intent of the drafters is not relevant when clear statutory language is used, writes Gorsuch: "This Court has explained many times over many years that, when the meaning of the statute's terms is plain, our job is at an end." Therefore, when the statute refers to sex, and that is the basis on which the plaintiffs were discriminated against, originalism is not a factor.

Justice Brett Kavanaugh, another justice appointed during the Trump administration, authored a dissent.[4] Justice Samuel Alito filed a separate dissent, joined by Justice Clarence Thomas.

One of the many questions that remain following this clear victory for LGBT rights is how this will impact religious liberty laws.

Many states have passed religious liberty statutes, and the court has considered the religious liberty claim on a national level. In *Masterpiece Cakeshop v. Colorado Civil Rights Commission*,[5] the court found that the Colorado Civil Rights Commission was hostile toward the religious objections of a cake-shop owner who refused services to a couple entering a same-sex marriage. In that case, the court was able to issue a narrow ruling that sidestepped the broader First Amendment issues of free exercise of religion and free speech. I am certain that more cases challenging these rights more directly will follow.

Regardless, civil rights proponents can claim a clear victory in this important workplace discrimination case that broadly expanded the rights of LGBT employees across the country.

Notes

1. Price Waterhouse v. Hopkins, 490 U.S. 228 (1989), Findlaw, https://caselaw.findlaw.com/us-supreme-court/490/228.html.
2. Oncale v. Sundowner Offshore Services, Inc., 523 U.S. 75 (1998), Oyez, https://www.oyez.org/cases/1997/96-568.
3. Jo Freeman, "How Sex Got into Title VII: Persistent Opportunism as a Maker of Public Policy," *Minnesota Journal of Law & Inequality* 9, no. 2 (1991): 163–84.
4. Bostock v. Clayton County, 590 U.S. ___ (2020), Oyez, https://www.oyez.org/cases/2019/17-1618.
5. Erwin Chemerinsky, "Not a Masterpiece: The Supreme Court's Decision in *Masterpiece Cakeshop v. Colorado Civil Rights Commission*," *Human Rights Magazine* 43, no. 4 (2018): 93–97, https://www.americanbar.org/groups/crsj/publications/human_rights_magazine_home/the-ongoing-challenge-to-define-free-speech/not-a-masterpiece/.

Chapter 29

Transgender Americans Still Face Workplace Discrimination despite Some Progress

GEORGE B. CUNNINGHAM

I'VE BEEN RESEARCHING DIVERSITY and inclusion in a variety of settings including sports and work for nearly two decades. The good news is that my work and that of my peers shows transgender individuals have made significant strides in the workplace. The bad news is that many hurdles remain to equal opportunity and an end to discrimination.

Signs of Progress

Various indicators point to meaningful improvements in access, treatment, and opportunities for transgender employees.

One such indicator is the Human Rights Campaign's Corporate Equality Index, an annual assessment of policies and benefits for LGBT individuals at Fortune 500 companies.[1] In 2002, only 3 percent of Fortune 500 companies had non-discrimination policies based on gender identity. That figure was 94 percent in the 2021 report. The report also shows that most Fortune 500 companies now include transgender-inclusive medical benefits. In 2002, no companies offered such provisions.

Another measure of how much things have changed is in the willingness of corporate giants and their CEOs to oppose policies that discriminate against transgender individuals. For instance, in 2018, then president Donald J. Trump said he would seek to legally define gender as immutably male or female. Coca-Cola, Apple, JPMorgan Chase, and dozens of other major US companies swiftly signaled their opposition.

Change is also evident from the backlash that has followed legislative efforts to limit the rights of transgender individuals to use public restrooms aligned with their gender identity. North Carolina, for example, was estimated to lose US$3.76 billion over a dozen years after companies nixed plans to build facilities in the state and performers canceled concerts because of the "bathroom bill" lawmakers passed. They later repealed it.

My own research with a colleague shows why corporate America is taking a stand: most consumers value inclusive-ness. Participants in a study we conducted in 2014 interpreted an LGBT-inclusive statement by an organization as a signal that it valued all forms of diversity. As a result, consumers' attraction to the organization increased.[2]

Hurdles Remain

Despite the progress, hurdles still exist, impeding full trans inclusion in the workplace.

A study I conducted with another colleague in 2017, for example, showed that, although attitudes toward transgender individuals have improved over time, they still lag behind perceptions toward lesbian, gay, and bisexual individuals.[3]

Legal scholars from UCLA's Williams Institute have shown that transgender people earn less and are more likely to be unemployed than their cisgender peers: those whose gender corresponds with their birth sex. In fact, in 2011, one in seven transgender individuals earned $10,000 or less a year, while the unemployment rate for trans people of color was nearly four times the national rate.

For those who are employed, they routinely face discrimination. In another study from the Williams Institute, state law and policy director Christy Mallory and colleagues found that more than one in four reported being fired, passed over for promotion, or not being hired in the past year because of their gender identity and expression.[4]

Others are aware of the mistreatment. In a survey of Texans, 79 percent of the respondents agreed that LGBT individuals face workplace discrimination.[5] Texans are not alone. According to the Movement Advancement Project, an organization whose mission is to promote equality for all, 48 percent of LGBT individuals live in states lacking employment protections based on sexual orientation or gender identity.[6]

More Inclusive Workplaces

The evidence suggests that transgender individuals have

made progress in the workplace, but they still face considerable barriers. What, then, can employers do to create more inclusive environments?

Legal protections are key. Organizational psychologists Laura Barron and Michelle Hebl have shown that the presence of antidiscrimination ordinances and laws decreases bias in employment decision-making.[7] Absent federal protections, states and cities can ensure all people have employment protections, irrespective of their gender identity and expression.

Organizational leaders also make a difference. My research shows that leader advocacy and role modeling are critical when creating and sustaining an inclusion culture.[8] Apple CEO Tim Cook, for example, has a history of strongly advocating for LGBT rights. It is little wonder, then, that Apple is routinely listed among the most LGBT-friendly companies.

Finally, coworkers play an important role, especially when they serve as allies. These are persons who advocate for transgender equality in the workplace and try to create welcoming, inclusive spaces. Allies seek to create social change, leading the charge at times and supporting their transgender colleagues in other instances.

Transgender inclusion helps all involved. Employees' engagement and performance improves, as does their psychological and physical health.[9] Diverse and inclusive organizations outperform their peers on objective measures of success, such as stock market performance. Thus, the path forward—one that clears the hurdles in place and creates an inclusive environment—is one that can benefit everyone.

Notes

1. "Corporate Equality Index 2021," Human Rights Campaign Foundation, https://reports.hrc.org/corporate-equality-index-2021.

2. George B. Cunningham and E. Nicole Melton, "Signals and Cues: LGBT Inclusive Advertising and Consumer Attraction," *Sport Marketing Quarterly* 23 (2014): 37–46, https://www.researchgate.net/publication/278035381_Signals_and_cues_LGBT_inclusive_advertising_and_consumer_attraction.

3. George B. Cunningham and Andrew C. Pickett, "Trans Prejudice in Sport: Differences from LGB Prejudice, the Influence of Gender, and Changes over Time," *Sex Roles* 78, nos. 3–4 (2018): 220–27, https://doi.org/10.1007/s11199-017-0791-6.

4. Christy Mallory, Andrew R. Flores, and Brad Sears, *Workplace Discrimination and Harassment against LGBT State and Local Government Employees* (Los Angeles: Williams Institute, UCLA School of Law, November 2021), https://williamsinstitute.law.ucla.edu/wp-content/uploads/Public-Sector-Discrimination-Nov-2021.pdf.

5. Christy Mallory, Taylor N. T. Brown, Stephen Russell, and Brad Sears, *The Impact of Stigma and Discrimination against LGBT People in Texas* (Los Angeles: Williams Institute, UCLA School of Law, April 2017), https://williamsinstitute.law.ucla.edu/wp-content/uploads/Impact-LGBT-Discrimination-TX-Apr-2017.pdf.

6. "Employment Nondiscrimination," State (tab), Movement Advancement Project, n.d., https://www.lgbtmap.org/equality-maps/employment_non_discrimination_laws.

7. Laura G. Barron and Michelle Hebl, "The Force of Law: The Effects of Sexual Orientation Antidiscrimination Legislation on Interpersonal Discrimination in Employment," *Psychology, Public Policy, and Law* 19, no. 2 (2013): 191–205, https://doi.org/10.1037/a0028350.

8. George B. Cunningham, "Creating and Sustaining Workplace Cultures Supportive of LGBT Employees in College Athletics," *Journal of Sport Management* 29, no. 4 (2015): 426–42, https://doi.org/10.1123/jsm.2014-0135.

9. Samantha R. Pflum, Rylan J. Testa, Kimberly F. Balsam, Peter B. Goldblum, and Bruce Bongar, "Social Support, Trans Community Connectedness, and Mental Health Symptoms among Transgender and Gender Nonconforming Adults," *Psychology of Sexual Orientation and Gender Diversity* 2, no. 3 (2015): 281–86, https://doi.org/10.1037/sgd0000122.

Chapter 30

Giving Birth as a Father— Experiences of Trans Birthing Parents

RUTH PEARCE*

THE UNITED KINGDOM'S HIGH COURT ruled in 2018 that Freddy McConnell, a man who gave birth to his child, does not have the right to be registered as a "father" on his child's birth certificate. At the time of this writing, McConnell, who is transgender, is planning to next take his case to the European Court of Human Rights.

At present, people who give birth to a child in the United

---

*Ruth Pearce cowrote this piece with colleagues from the Trans Pregnancy project: Sally Hines, Carla Pfeffer, Damien W. Riggs, Elisabetta Ruspini, and Francis Ray White.

Kingdom are registered as the "mother." However, this does not accurately reflect the lived reality of a growing number of transgender birth parents and can therefore create inconsistencies. For example, McConnell is, for all other social and legal purposes, a man. As his legal team note, "Freddy is legally a man and his legal papers display the same."[1]

As a researcher, I work for the Trans Pregnancy project, an international study examining trans and nonbinary people's experiences of pregnancy and childbirth.[2] We conducted in-depth interviews with 52 people about their experiences of pregnancy in Australia, Bulgaria, Canada, Germany, the United States, and the United Kingdom. We have also spoken to young trans and nonbinary people who are considering their options for parenthood as well as medical professionals working with these groups. We found that birth parents seek forms of legal recognition that are consistent with how they experience gender in their everyday life.

Giving Birth as a Man

Many trans people undertake a social or medical transition that does not involve surgery to remove their reproductive organs.[3] Therefore transition does not necessarily take away the ability or desire to reproduce. As Jonathan,* a participant in our research, argued, "I do want a child that's biologically mine, and I can get pregnant . . . I do have the ability to do that, so why should I not make use of that?"

It is not just trans men who might choose to become pregnant. This can also be an option for many nonbinary or

---

*The names of research participants Jonathan, Joseph, and Stefan are pseudonyms to protect their privacy.

genderqueer people: that is, individuals whose gender is partly or entirely separate from the binary options of female or male.

Trans people may conceive in a variety of ways: through intercourse, sperm donation, or assisted reproductive technologies.[4] If a trans person is taking testosterone, it is typical for them to pause their medication regime some months before they conceive. There are, however, cases of people becoming unintentionally pregnant while undergoing hormone therapy, as testosterone is not a reliable contraceptive.

More Common Than You May Think

There are no firm statistics available on the number of trans and nonbinary people who become pregnant and give birth. However, our research indicates that a growing number of trans people are choosing to start their own families in this way. More than 7,000 people worldwide are members of a private social media group for trans people who give birth.

In Australia, 262 men are recorded to have given birth between 2012 and 2021.[5] In England, the findings of the Maternity Survey 2021 indicate that at least 131 trans people gave birth in February alone.[6] As research participant Joseph explained, "It's not a new story, it's not sensational."

Modern Families

Some of the reporting on McConnell's case in the British media used quite emotive language. In stating that his child may be "without mother," the implication was that something important might be lost.

But many children have been born to men and nonbinary people. Some are in relationships with women who become the mothers of their children, while others are single or in relationships with other men or nonbinary people. There are many reasons why, in fact, children might grow up without a mother: if their mother dies in childbirth, if they are raised solely by male relatives, or if they are adopted by a male couple or single male parent. What is missing from the reporting on the McConnell case is an account of what has been gained. Children gain a loving parent, and the parents gain an addition to their family.

A Difficult Road Forward

Participants in our study reported a range of different experiences and views on matters such as gender, parenthood, and being trans or nonbinary. Nevertheless, all emphasized the importance of recognizing that some people who give birth may be fathers or nonbinary parents.

Trans and nonbinary birth parents want fair and equitable access to social and health care services and to have their experiences respected. When pregnancy is conceptualized as something that can only happen to women, then men and nonbinary people can be excluded from services and legal protections, with potentially tragic consequences.[7]

Many participants in our study emphasized their fears around registering their child's birth. It is possible for a birth parent to be registered as the "father" or simply the "parent" of their child in countries such as Sweden and in some Canadian provinces and US states. However, participants in countries such as the United Kingdom and Germany described difficulties associated with being forced to register as the "mother" of their child. For example, Stefan had expressed anxious uncertainty to the registrar: "How I should demonstrate or prove or verify that he's my son with this birth certificate, because nobody would believe me."

For these people, having their gender appropriately recorded on their child's birth certificate is a matter of basic dignity. But mostly importantly, it is a matter of safety for the child. Parents such as Stefan echoed McConnell, who has stated that "protecting my child has always been . . . my number one concern."[8] In expressing fears for the future of their children, they note the potential confusion that can arise from a child's documentation being inconsistent with that of their parents.

Family forms and structures have changed many times through history and are still changing. Families with trans parents exist, and they are here to stay. It is incumbent upon us to do what we can to understand the unique characteristics, needs, challenges, and strengths of these 21st-century families.

Notes

1. Karen Holden, "Updated Press Release," A City Law Firm, July 19, 2019, https://acitylawfirm.com/opinion-the-law-must-change-to-reflect-true -equality-for-transgender-rights/.
2. Trans Pregnancy (website), University of Leeds, https://transpregnancy .leeds.ac.uk/.
3. Juno Obedin-Maliver and Harvey J. Makadon, "Transgender Men and Pregnancy," *Obstetric Medicine* vol. 9, no. 1 (2015): 4–8, https://doi .org/10.1177/1753495x15612658.
4. Alexis D. Light, Juno Obedin-Maliver, Jae M. Sevelius, and Jennifer L. Kerns, "Transgender Men Who Experienced Pregnancy after Female-to-Male Gender Transitioning," *Obstetrics & Gynecology* 124, no. 6 (2014): 1120–27, https://doi.org/10.1097/aog.0000000000000540.
5. "Medicare Item Reports," Services Australia, last updated April 27, 2022, http://medicarestatistics.humanservices.gov.au/statistics/mbs_item.jsp.
6. *Maternity Survey 2021*, Care Quality Commission, 2022, https://www .cqc.org.uk/publications/surveys/maternity-survey-2021.
7. Daphna Stroumsa, Elizabeth F. S. Roberts, Hadrian Kinnear, and Lisa H. Harris, "The Power and Limits of Classification—a 32-Year-Old Man with Abdominal Pain," *New England Journal of Medicine* 380, no. 20 (2019): 1885–88, https://doi.org/10.1056/nejmp1811491.
8. Robert Booth, "Transgender Man Who Gave Birth Loses High Court Privacy Ruling," *Guardian*, July 16, 2019, https://www.theguardian.com /society/2019/jul/16/transgender-man-who-gave-birth-loses-high -court-privacy-case-fred-mcconnell.

Chapter 31

Gender Is Personal—Not Computational

FOAD HAMIDI, MORGAN KLAUS SCHEUERMAN, and STACY BRANHAM

IMAGINE WALKING down the street and seeing advertising screens change their content based on how you walk, how you talk, or even the shape of your chest. These screens rely on hidden cameras, microphones, and computers to guess if you're male or female. This might sound futuristic, but patrons at a Norwegian pizzeria discovered that's exactly what was happening: women were seeing ads for salad, and men were seeing ads for meat options. The software running a digital advertising board spilled the beans when it crashed and displayed its underlying code. The motivation behind using this technology might have been to improve advertising quality or user experience. Nevertheless, many customers were unpleasantly surprised by it.

This sort of situation is not just creepy and invasive. It's worse: efforts at automatic gender recognition—using algorithms to guess a person's gender based on still images, video, or audio—raise significant social and ethical concerns that are not yet fully explored.[1] Most current research on automatic gender recognition technologies focuses instead on technological details.

Our research has found that people with diverse gender identities, including those identifying as transgender or gender nonbinary, are particularly concerned that these systems could miscategorize them,[2] thereby undermining their efforts to curate and control their gender presentation in digital systems.[3] People who express their gender differently from stereotypical male and female norms already experience discrimination and harm as a result of being miscategorized or misunderstood.[4] Ideally, technology designers should develop systems to make these problems less common, not more so.

Using Algorithms to Classify People

As digital technologies become more powerful and sophisticated, their designers are trying to use them to identify and categorize complex human characteristics, such as sexual orientation, gender, and ethnicity. The idea is that with enough training on abundant user data, algorithms can learn to analyze people's appearance and behavior—and perhaps one day characterize people as well as, or even better than, other humans do.

Gender is a hard topic for people to handle. It's a complex concept with important roles both as a cultural construct and a core aspect of an individual's identity. Researchers, scholars, and activists are increasingly revealing the diverse, fluid, and multifaceted aspects of gender. In the process, they find that ignoring this diversity can lead to both harmful experiences and social injustice.

For example, according to the 2016 National Transgender Survey, 47 percent of transgender participants stated that they had experienced some form of discrimination at their workplace due to their gender identity. More than half of transgender people who were harassed, assaulted, or expelled because of their gender identity had attempted suicide.

Many people have, at one time or another, been surprised or confused or even angered to find themselves mistaken for a person of another gender. When that happens to someone who is transgender—as an estimated 0.6 percent of Americans, or 1.4 million people, are—it can cause considerable stress and anxiety.

Effects of Automatic Gender Recognition

In our research, we interviewed 13 transgender and gender-nonconforming people about their general impressions of automatic gender recognition technology. We also asked them to describe their responses to imaginary future scenarios where they might encounter it. All 13 participants were worried about this technology and doubted whether it could offer their community any benefits.

Of particular concern was the prospect of being misgendered by it; in their experience, gender is largely an internal, subjective characteristic, not something that is necessarily or entirely expressed outwardly. Therefore, neither humans nor algorithms can accurately read gender through physical features, such as the face, body, or voice. They described how being misgendered by algorithms could potentially feel worse than if humans did it. Technology is often perceived to be objective and unbiased, so being wrongly categorized by an algorithm would bolster the misconception that a transgender identity is inauthentic. One participant described how they would feel hurt if a "million-dollar piece of software developed by however many people" decided that they are not who they themselves believe they are.

Subsequent research revealed that participant concerns were not unfounded. Not only do computer vision researchers not engage deeply with their definitions or sources of gender,[5] commercial gender classification technology—deployed by some of the largest tech companies in the world—misgenders transgender people more often than cisgender people do.[6]

Privacy and Transparency

The people we interviewed shared the common public concern that automated cameras could be used for surveillance without their consent or knowledge; for years, researchers and activists have raised red flags about increasing threats to privacy in a world populated by sensors and cameras.

But our participants described how the effects of these technologies could be greater for transgender people. For instance, they might be singled out as unusual because they look or behave differently from what the underlying algorithms expect. Some participants were even concerned that systems might falsely determine that they are trying to be someone else to deceive the system.

Their concerns also extended to cisgender people who might look or act differently from the majority, such as people of different races, people the algorithms perceive to be androgynous, and people with unique facial structures. This already happens to people from minority racial and ethnic backgrounds, who are regularly misidentified by facial recognition technology. For example, existing facial recognition technology in some cameras fails to properly detect the faces of Asian users and send messages asking them to stop blinking or to open their eyes.

Our interviewees wanted to know more about how automatic gender recognition systems work and what they're used for. They didn't want to know deep technical details but did want to make sure the technology would not compromise their privacy or identity. They also wanted more transgender people involved in the early stages of design and development of these systems, well before they are deployed.

Creating Inclusive Automatic Systems

Our research results demonstrate how designers of automatic categorization technologies can inadvertently cause harm by making assumptions about the simplicity and predictability of human characteristics. Our research adds to a growing body of work that attempts to incorporate gender into technology more thoughtfully.

Minorities have historically been left out of conversations about large-scale technology deployment, including ethnic minorities and people with disabilities. Yet scientists and designers alike know that including input from minority groups during the design process can lead to technical innovations that benefit all people. We advocate for a more gender-inclusive and human-centric approach to automation that incorporates diverse perspectives.

As digital technologies develop and mature, they can lead to impressive innovations. But as humans direct that work, they should avoid amplifying human biases and prejudices that are negative and limiting. In the case of automatic gender recognition, we do not necessarily conclude that these algorithms should be abandoned. Rather, designers of these systems should be inclusive of, and sensitive to, the diversity and complexity of human identity.

Notes

1. Feng Lin, Yingxiao Wu, Yan Zhuang, Xi Long, and Wenyao Xu, "Human Gender Classification: A Review," *International Journal of Biometrics* 8, nos. 3/4 (2016): 275–300, https://doi.org/10.1504/ijbm.2016.082604.
2. Foad Hamidi, Morgan Klaus Scheuerman, and Stacy M. Branham, "Gender Recognition or Gender Reductionism? The Social Implications of Embedded Gender Recognition Systems," *Proceedings of the 2018 CHI Conference on Human Factors in Computing Systems*, April 2018, paper 8, 1–13, https://doi.org/10.1145/3173574.3173582.
3. Morgan Klaus Scheuerman, Stacy M. Branham, and Foad Hamidi, "Safe Spaces and Safe Places: Unpacking Technology-Mediated Experiences of Safety and Harm with Transgender People," *Proceedings of the ACM on Human-Computer Interaction* 2, no. CSCW (November 2018): article no. 155, 1–27, https://doi.org/10.1145/3274424.
4. Kevin A. McLemore, "Experiences with Misgendering: Identity Misclassification of Transgender Spectrum Individuals," *Self and Identity* 14, no. 1 (2014): 51–74, https://doi.org/10.1080/15298868.2014.950691.
5. Morgan Klaus Scheuerman, Kandrea Wade, Caitlin Lustig, and Jed R. Brubaker, "How We've Taught Algorithms to See Identity: Constructing Race and Gender in Image Databases for Facial Analysis," *Proceedings of the ACM on Human-Computer Interaction* 4, no. CSCW1 (May 2020): article no. 58, 1–35, https://doi.org/10.1145/3392866.
6. Morgan Klaus Scheuerman, Jacob M. Paul, and Jed R. Brubaker, "How Computers See Gender: An Evaluation of Gender Classification in Commercial Facial Analysis Services," *Proceedings of the ACM on Human-Computer Interaction* 3, no. CSCW (November 2019): article no. 144, 1–33, https://doi.org/10.1145/3359246.

Chapter 32

Transgender Americans Are More Likely to Be Unemployed and Poor

CHRISTOPHER CARPENTER and GILBERT GONZALES

IN A LANDMARK DECISION, the United States Supreme Court ruled in 2020 that gay men, lesbian women, bisexual individuals, and transgender people—individuals whose sex assigned at birth does not match their current immanent sense of being male, female, both, or neither—cannot be discriminated against in the workplace simply because of their sexual orientation or gender identity.[1] The decision involved three separate but related cases: two involving men who were fired for being gay and one involving a transgender woman, Aimee Stephens, who was fired from her job at a funeral home after her transition.[2] The court's ruling in favor of Stephens affects the estimated 1.4 million adults in the United States who identify as transgender.[3] Stephens passed away on May 12, 2020, just one month before the Supreme Court ruled in her favor.

A study we published on February 11, 2020, suggests that nondiscrimination protections for transgender people are likely to be especially meaningful.[4] As scholars of economics, health, and LGBT populations, we wanted to find out about how transgender people fare economically. We learned that on nearly all measures of economic and social well-being, they do much worse than the general population.

Little Is Known about Transgender People

A growing body of research on sexual minorities has steadily advanced over the past 25 years. However, when we first started working on this research project in 2017, we found little published work on the economic lives of transgender people.

Most research that did exist came from studies of only one or two progressive-leaning states, such as California or Massachusetts, or used "convenience" or "snowball" samples of transgender people where participants were recruited through social networks.[5] These types of data are useful, but they might not accurately reflect the general transgender population in the United States.

What We Found

This is where our study came in. We used data from an annual telephone survey of over 400,000 individuals in the United

States that asks people about their employment, income, health insurance coverage, and overall health. It's called the Behavioral Risk Factor Surveillance System of the Centers for Disease Control and Prevention.[6]

Starting in 2014, this survey gave states the option to ask respondents about their sexual orientation and gender identity. When the question "Are you transgender?" was asked, over 2,100 adults responded "yes." Although this is only a fraction of 1 percent of the total survey sample, it is a much larger sample of transgender people than has been used in other survey-based studies. And, importantly, it allowed us to study transgender individuals from states as diverse as Pennsylvania, Oklahoma, Idaho, and Florida.

The most consistent pattern we found is that individuals who described themselves as transgender did much worse in aspects of their lives that affect their economic well-being—like educational attainment, employment, and poverty status—than otherwise comparable individuals who did not identify as transgender. This was especially true for employment. Transgender people were 11 percentage points less likely to be working compared with nontransgender, or cisgender, people.

We found that this effect was driven by two forces: transgender people were more likely to be unemployed—that is, they would like to work but are not currently working—and much more likely to report that they are unable to work.

The data don't tell us why transgender people may be unable to work. It may be due to a disability, poor health, lack of transportation, or other structural barriers. It's also possible that transgender people have been turned away so many

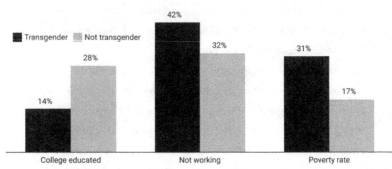

Transgender Americans.

Transgender | Not transgender

College educated: Transgender 14%, Not transgender 28%
Not working: Transgender 42%, Not transgender 32%
Poverty rate: Transgender 31%, Not transgender 17%

times by potential employers—possibly due to discrimination, which is now illegal throughout the United States—that they are what economists aptly refer to as "discouraged"; thus they report that they are "unable to (find) work."

Our results also showed that transgender people had much lower rates of college education than nontransgender people. While 28 percent of nontransgender people in the survey said they had a college education, the same was true for only 14 percent of transgender respondents.

Even after accounting for lower college education rates, we found that transgender people had higher rates of poverty and worse health than otherwise comparable individuals who did not identify as transgender.

Rapidly Changing Policy

Of course, there are limits to the Supreme Court's decision, and LGBT rights advocates have already stressed the need to adopt a federal Equality Act, which would extend nondiscrimination protections to housing, public accommodations,

In a survey of 400,000 Americans in 2014–2015,
those who said they were transgender were more likely to report
that they were poor, not working, and not college educated.
*The Conversation, CC BY-ND. Data from the Centers for Disease Control
and Prevention's Behavioral Risk Factor Surveillance System*

education, and health care—all areas of life that are currently
not explicitly protected by federal civil rights law for LGBT
people. The need for these protections was highlighted by
the timing of the Supreme Court decision in 2020: just three
days prior to the ruling, the Health and Human Services Office
for Civil Rights rolled back nondiscrimination protections for
transgender people in health care that were instituted by the
prior presidential administration.

Notes

1. Bostock v. Clayton County, 590 U.S. ___ (2020), Oyez, https://www.oyez .org/cases/2019/17-1618.
2. R.G. & G.R. Harris Funeral Homes Inc. v. Equal Employment Opportunity Commission, 590 U.S. ___ (2020), Oyez, https://www.oyez.org/cases /2019/18-107.
3. Andrew R. Flores, Jody L. Herman, Gary J. Gates, and Taylor N. T. Brown, *How Many Adults Identify as Transgender in the United States?* Williams Institute, UCLA School of Law, June 2016, https://williamsinstitute.law .ucla.edu/publications/trans-adults-united-states/.
4. Christopher S. Carpenter, Samuel T. Eppink, and Gilbert Gonzales, "Transgender Status, Gender Identity, and Socioeconomic Outcomes in the United States," *ILR Review* 73, no. 3 (2020): 573–99, https://doi .org/10.1177/0019793920902776.
5. Jaime M. Grant, Lisa A. Mottet, and Justin Tanis with Jack Harrison, Jody L. Herman, and Mara Keisling, *Injustice at Every Turn: A Report of the National Transgender Discrimination Survey U.S. Transgender Survey* (Washington, DC: National Center for Transgender Equality and National Gay and Lesbian Task Force, 2011), https://transequality.org/issues /us-trans-survey.
6. "Behavioral Risk Factor Surveillance System Centers," Centers for Disease Control and Prevention, last reviewed May 4, 2022, https://www .cdc.gov/brfss/index.html.

Chapter 33

How High School Sports Became the Latest Battleground over Transgender Rights

ELIZABETH A. SHARROW

THE RIGHT OF GIRLS AND WOMEN to compete on sports teams has endured 50 years of policy debate. With more young people now publicly identifying as transgender,[1] whether transgender girls can compete on girls' high school teams has come to the forefront of these discussions. My research helps explain why sports is a key site for disputes over transgender equality today.[2] The expansion of competitive sports for girls and women—both internationally and in the United States—has heightened scrutiny of who "belongs" on girls' and women's teams.

A Patchwork of Rules

Whether transgender youth can participate in interscholastic athletics currently depends on where they live. Some states, like Minnesota and Massachusetts, allow transgender athletes to compete on the teams that comport with their identity, regardless of medical interventions. Others, like Illinois and Virginia, require a documented medical transition, including disclosure of hormone therapies. In states such as Georgia and New Mexico, athletic eligibility is determined by the sex designated on a student's birth certificate. Still others, like Pennsylvania, let local schools decide.

These eligibility rules are typically determined by state athletic associations, not state legislatures. However, in recent years states have stepped up efforts to ban transgender youth from participating in high school and college sports. As of early 2022, 13 states banned trans athletes as a matter of law.

Title IX and Same-Sex Sports

Title IX of the Education Amendments of 1972 is a federal law that bans sex discrimination at all levels of education. Every US school must comply with the mandate. Title IX has dramatically increased women's access to college education, graduate schools, and athletics. As of 2019, 43 percent of high school athletes were girls, as compared with 7 percent in 1971, the year before the bill became law. After Title IX passed, policy makers had to decide how to increase women's access to school-sponsored sports.

The National Organization for Women and other pro-integration activists argued that coed teams would ultimately help secure women's equal status and visibility as athletes. At the same time, they worried that immediate sex integration might disadvantage women, given the previous lack of training, coaching, and athletic competition for girls and women. So, starting in 1979, policy makers required that schools expand access by creating new teams specifically for women and girls.

Since then, women have rarely competed on men's college or high school sports teams. Likewise, in 13 cases between 1971 and 2006, US courts ruled against cisgender boys and men—those assigned male at birth and who live as boys and men—who wanted to play on teams for girls and women. Research shows that the legal reasoning in these cases advances the dubious notion that girls are inherently inferior athletes.[3]

Despite controversy around sex-segregated teams, they remain the norm for athletic competition in the United States.

Currently, transgender athletes are underrepresented at the high school level. One 2017 report from the Human Rights Campaign found that only 12 percent of transgender girls participated in organized sports, compared with 68 percent of young people overall. Among the reasons for this is a lack of clarity in equity policy. Court cases have established that public schools must affirm the gender of all students and protect them against exclusion under Title IX. However, the rights of transgender athletes to access high school sports teams are not specifically addressed in federal athletic policy guidelines.

Transgender Visibility and Backlash

Over the past three decades, the movement for transgender rights has made many legislative and social gains. These include increased public recognition, legal victories, and some state-level protections against discrimination at school. But increased visibility for transgender people has also provoked legislative backlash on issues like access to public restrooms.

These "bathroom bills," which included attempts to deny transgender students access to sex-segregated bathrooms at school, provided a blueprint for a number of legislative proposals barring transgender athletes. They were premised on the idea that transgender people should not have the right to use sex-segregated spaces, like public restrooms and locker rooms, that align with their gender identity.

International Sports and Sex Testing

Ongoing disputes in the international sports environment are also relevant to the debate about who "belongs" in women's sports.

The case of South African Olympic track star Caster Semenya drew significant attention to this question. Semenya is a cisgender woman—meaning she was assigned female at birth and lives as a woman—and an Olympic gold medalist in the women's 800-meter event. After her first international championship in 2009, several competitors challenged her victory. They suggested that she was too fast, that her physical appearance was not sufficiently feminine, and that she was not "actually a woman."

In a decade-long dispute, the international governing agency for track and field fought to enact a contested policy that required Semenya—and any other woman athlete whose gender was questioned—to submit to bodily and hormonal evaluations and possible medical treatments in order to remain eligible for particular running events. The policy was later abandoned. These sex testing policies, also known as gender verification, have long policed the elite women's category and particularly harm women of color, who have been disproportionately scrutinized.[4]

Meanwhile, scientists are divided on whether monitoring testosterone—as advocated by both international policy and multiple contested state laws banning trans athletes—can identify any consistent athletic advantage. They continue to debate the meanings of gender and the impacts of sex difference. As policy makers and elected officials debate the future of sports for girls and women, the rights of transgender athletes hang in the balance.

Notes

1. Tey Meadow, *Trans Kids: Being Gendered in the Twenty-First Century* (Berkeley: University of California Press, 2018.
2. Elizabeth A. Sharrow, "'Female Athlete' Politic: Title IX and the Naturalization of Sex Difference in Public Policy," *Politics, Groups, and Identities* 5, no. 1 (2017): 46–66, https://doi.org/10.1080/21565503 .2016.1268178; Elizabeth A. Sharrow, "Sports, Transgender Rights and the Bodily Politics of Cisgender Supremacy," *Laws* 10, no. 3 (2021): 63, https://doi.org/10.3390/laws10030063.
3. Adam Love and Kimberly Kelly, "Equity or Essentialism? U.S. Courts and the Legitimation of Girls' Teams in High School Sport," *Gender & Society* 25, no. 2 (2011): 227–49, https://doi.org/10.1177/0891243211398866.
4. Katrina Karkazis and Rebecca M. Jordan-Young, "The Powers of Testosterone: Obscuring Race and Regional Bias in the Regulation of Women Athletes," *Feminist Formations* 30, no. 2 (2018): 1–39, https://doi .org/10.1353/ff.2018.0017.

Chapter 34

How the Olympics Shifted Away from Testosterone Tests and toward Human Rights

RYAN STORR, MADELEINE PAPE, and SHEREE BEKKER*

IN NOVEMBER 2021, the International Olympic Committee (IOC) released a much-anticipated policy document aimed at making the Olympics more inclusive for transgender athletes and athletes with sex variations. The IOC framework builds on more than two years of consultation with diverse athletes, advocates, and stakeholders.[1]

---

*Independent researcher Payoshni Mitra contributed to this chapter.

New Zealand's Laurel Hubbard, who is transgender,
competed at the Tokyo Olympics in 2021.
AP Photo / Mark Schiefelbein

One of the most prominent gender equity and human rights issues of recent years has been the inclusion of gender-minoritized people—those whose bodies and/or gender expression and identity do not neatly align with normative notions of the female/male binary. This issue affects sport globally, from grassroots to elite levels. Stakeholders have long called for change.

We work with sports organizations and athletes grappling with the question of inclusion in women's sport. Our own research has highlighted that many sports organizations develop policies with little to no knowledge of the complexity of the issue—and often without engaging the athletes affected.[2]

The IOC framework follows a long and much-critiqued history of efforts to define the boundaries of the female athlete category, dating back to the "nude parades" of the 1960s. In the past, the goal was to find a "biological basis of womanhood" while relying on incomplete and controversial scientific evidence.[3] Today, however, there is wider recognition of the fact that science alone cannot provide a straightforward answer to such a socially and biologically complex question. An alternative approach, reflected in the IOC's framework, is to build policy around the concept of human rights.

What Does the IOC Framework Say?

The framework recognizes human rights as a fundamental responsibility of sports governing bodies. It explicitly takes the

approach that athletes shouldn't be excluded solely on the basis of their transgender identity or sex variations. The framework sets out 10 principles to guide the policy development process:

1. Inclusion of everyone without prejudice against their gender or sex-linked traits
2. Prevention of harm
3. Nondiscrimination
4. Fairness
5. No presumption of advantage
6. Evidence-based approaches to regulation
7. The primacy of health and bodily autonomy
8. A stakeholder-centered approach to rule development
9. The right to privacy
10. Periodic review of eligibility regulations

Importantly, the framework attempts to move sports governing bodies away from relying on testosterone as a one-size-fits-all measure of eligibility. The relationship between testosterone and performance is so complex that sports governing bodies cannot realistically expect to rely on testosterone measures when defining eligibility. There is just as much diversity among the bodies and performances of trans women and women with sex variations as we see among cisgender and normatively bodied women athletes.

The IOC's spokespeople were pragmatic: let's take one step at a time, have faith in the 10 principles, and see where they take us. In this way, the framework (and its underlying philosophy) moves us well beyond contentious testosterone thresholds introduced in 2015,[4] as well as the 2003 Stockholm consensus,[5] which required athletes to have had affirmation surgeries and "anatomical changes."

In fact, the IOC now recognizes the "severe harm" and systemic discrimination caused by such eligibility criteria and policies.[6] This includes the disproportionate burdens and harms that have been wrought upon women of color from Global South nations in sports like track and field.

The question now is this: How will other sports governing bodies, most notably the international federations that govern each Olympic sport, be brought on side? The IOC now calls for international federations to take "a principled approach to develop their criteria that are applicable to their sport."[7]

An Important and Welcome Move

This framework represents a step forward for gender-inclusive sport, but there's more work ahead. It doesn't mention nonbinary athletes at all, meaning it still frames elite sports participation within a strict gender binary.

It's promising to see a shift away from a paradigm focused on particular scientific and medical approaches regulating exclusion of certain groups. The move toward a contemporary vision of gender-inclusive sport gives reason for optimism. This approach is a positive move for gender-equitable sport; both trans women and women with sex variations will be valuable allies in the fight to make sport safe and inclusive for all women.

We hope it will help make grassroots a more welcome space for trans and gender-diverse people. These groups report alarming levels of poor mental health and suicidal ideation and have a right to enjoy opportunities to improve their well-being through sport. Sport has a unique opportunity to advance progress and health outcomes for marginalized communities. This move forward may offer hope to young people of diverse genders and sex so that they too can strive to achieve greatness in a sport they love.

Notes

1. International Olympic Committee, *IOC Framework on Fairness, Inclusion and Non-discrimination on the Basis of Gender Identity and Sex Variations*, 2021, https://stillmed.olympics.com/media/Documents/News/2021/11/IOC-Framework-Fairness-Inclusion-Non-discrimination-2021.pdf?_ga=2.23770618.1919307062.1637103265-221083472.1637103265.
2. L. Stewart, P. O'Halloran, J. Oates, E. Sherry, and R. Storr, "Developing Trans-Athlete Policy in Australian National Sport Organizations," *International Journal of Sport Policy and Politics* 13, no. 4 (2021): 565–85, https://doi.org/10.1080/19406940.2021.1955727.
3. Madeleine Pape, "Expertise and Non-binary Bodies: Sex, Gender and the Case of Dutee Chand," *Body & Society* 25, no. 4 (2019): 3–28, https://doi.org/10.1177/1357034x19865940.
4. International Olympic Committee, *IOC Consensus Meeting on Sex Reassignment and Hyperandrogenism*, November 2015, https://

stillmed.olympic.org/Documents/Commissions_PDFfiles/Medical
_commission/2015-11_ioc_consensus_meeting_on_sex_reassignment
_and_hyperandrogenism-en.pdf.

5. *Statement of the Stockholm Consensus on Sex Reassignment in Sports*,
2003, https://stillmed.olympic.org/Documents/Reports/EN/en_report
_905.pdf.

6. Sheree Bekker and Anna Posbergh, "Safeguarding in Sports Settings:
Unpacking a Conflicting Identity," *Qualitative Research in Sport, Exercise
and Health* 14, no. 2 (2021): 181–98, https://doi.org/10.1080/2159676x
.2021.1920456.

7. International Olympic Committee, *IOC Framework.*

Suggested Supplementary Reading

These suggestions for further reading introduce some of the cutting-edge and enduring reference texts related to the topics covered in this book, both from peer-reviewed, academic trans studies and from works for a general audience. They are organized by theme.

Introductory Texts on Gender Diversity and Trans Experiences

Bornstein, Kate. *My Gender Workbook.* New York: Routledge, 1997.
———. *A Queer and Pleasant Danger: A Memoir.* New York: Penguin Random House, 2013.
Faye, Shon. *The Transgender Issue: An Argument for Justice.* London: Penguin Random House, 2021.
Feinberg, Leslie. *Stone Butch Blues.* 20th anniversary author's ed. 2014. Available for free online: https://www.lesliefeinberg.net.
———. *Transgender Warriors: Making History from Joan of Arc to Marsha P. Johnson and Beyond.* 25th anniversary ed. Boston: Beacon Press, 2021.
Gossett, Reina, Eric A. Stanley, and Johanna Burton, eds. *Trap Door: Trans Cultural Production and the Politics of Visibility.* Cambridge, MA: MIT Press, 2017.
Jacques, Juliet. *Trans: A Memoir.* New York: Verso Books, 2016.
Mock, Janet. *Redefining Realness: My Path to Womanhood, Identity, Love & So Much More.* New York: Atria Books, 2014.

Serano, Julia. *Whipping Girl: A Transsexual Woman on Sexism and the Scapegoating of Femininity*. 2nd ed. Berkeley, CA: Seal Press, 2016.

Stockton, Kathryn Bond. *Gender(s)*. Cambridge, MA: MIT Press, 2021.

Stryker, Susan. *Transgender History: The Roots of Today's Revolution*. 2nd ed. Berkeley, CA: Seal Press, 2017.

Sullivan, Lou. *We Both Laughed in Pleasure: The Selected Diaries of Lou Sullivan, 1961–1991*. Edited by Ellis Martin and Zach Oma. New York: Nightboat Books, 2019.

Tourmaline. "Filmmaker and Activist Tourmaline on How to Freedom Dream." *Vogue*, July 2, 2020. https://www.vogue.com/article/filmmaker-and-activist-tourmaline-on-how-to-freedom-dream.

Valentine, David. *Imagining Transgender: An Ethnography of a Category*. Durham, NC: Duke University Press, 2007.

Williams, Rachel Anne. *Transgressive: A Trans Woman on Gender, Feminism, and Politics*. Philadelphia: Jessica Kingsley Publishers, 2019.

Trans and Gender History in the United States and Europe

Chauncey, George. *Gay New York: Gender, Urban Culture, and the Making of the Gay Male World, 1890–1940*. New York: Basic Books, 2019.

DeVun, Leah. *The Shape of Sex: Nonbinary Gender from Genesis to the Renaissance*. New York: Columbia University Press, 2021.

Dose, Ralf. *Magnus Hirschfeld: The Origins of the Gay Liberation Movement*. Translated by Edward H. Willis. New York: Monthly Review Press, 2014.

Duberman, Martin. *Stonewall: The Definitive Story of the LGBTQ Rights Uprising That Changed America*. New York: Plume, 2019.

Faderman, Lillian, and Stuart Timmons. *Gay L.A.: A History of Sexual Outlaws, Power Politics, and Lipstick Lesbians*. New York: Basic Books, 2006.

Heaney, Emma. *The New Woman: Literary Modernism, Queer Theory, and the Trans Feminine Allegory*. Evanston, IL: Northwestern University Press, 2017.

Kunzel, Regina. *Criminal Intimacy: Prison and the Uneven History of Modern American Sexuality*. Chicago: University of Chicago Press, 2010.

LaFleur, Greta, Masha Raskolnikov, and Anna Klosowska, eds. *Trans Historical: Gender Plurality before the Modern*. Ithaca, NY: Cornell University Press, 2021.

Manion, Jen. *Female Husbands: A Trans History*. Cambridge: Cambridge University Press, 2021.

Meyerowitz, Joanne. *How Sex Changed: A History of Transsexuality in the United States*. New ed. Cambridge, MA: Harvard University Press, 2004.

Newton, Esther. *Mother Camp: Female Impersonators in America*. Phoenix ed. Chicago: University of Chicago Press, 1979.

Sears, Clare. *Arresting Dress: Cross-Dressing, Law, and Fascination in Nine-teenth-Century San Francisco*. Durham, NC: Duke University Press, 2014.

Skidmore, Emily. *True Sex: The Lives of Trans Men at the Turn of the Twen-tieth Century*. Reprint, New York: New York University Press, 2019.

Law, Policy, and Government

Beauchamp, Toby. *Going Stealth: Transgender Politics and U.S. Surveillance Practices*. Durham, NC: Duke University Press Books, 2019.

Currah, Paisley. *Sex Is as Sex Does: Governing Transgender Identity*. New York: New York University Press, 2022.

Davis, Heath Fogg. *Beyond Trans: Does Gender Matter?* New York: New York University Press, 2018.

McDonald, CeCe. " 'Go beyond Our Natural Selves': The Prison Letters of CeCe McDonald." *TSQ: Transgender Studies Quarterly* 4, no. 2 (May 1, 2017): 243–65.

Spade, Dean. *Normal Life: Administrative Violence, Critical Trans Politics, and the Limits of Law*. Revised, expanded ed. Durham, NC: Duke University Press Books, 2015.

Stanley, Eric A. *Atmospheres of Violence: Structuring Antagonism and the Trans/Queer Ungovernable*. Durham, NC: Duke University Press Books, 2021.

Stanley, Eric A., and Nat Smith, eds. *Captive Genders: Trans Embodiment and the Prison Industrial Complex*. 2nd ed. Oakland, CA: AK Press, 2015.

Stryker, Susan. "On Stalling and Turning: A Wayward Genealogy for a Binary-Abolitionist Public Toilet Project." *Social Text* 39, no. 3 (September 1, 2021): 37–54.

Transgender Health Care and Science

Fausto-Sterling, Anne. *Sexing the Body: Gender Politics and the Construction of Sexuality*. Revised ed. New York: Basic Books, 2020.

Germon, Jennifer. *Gender: A Genealogy of an Idea*. New York: Palgrave Macmillan, 2009.

Malatino, Hil. *Side Affects: On Being Trans and Feeling Bad*. Minneapolis: University of Minnesota Press, 2022.

———. *Trans Care*. Minneapolis: University of Minnesota Press, 2020.

Richardson, Sarah S. *Sex Itself: The Search for Male and Female in the Human Genome*. Chicago: University of Chicago Press, 2015.

Roughgarden, Joan. *Evolution's Rainbow: Diversity, Gender, and Sexuality in Nature and People*. 10th anniversary ed. Berkeley: University of California Press, 2013.

shuster, stef m. *Trans Medicine: The Emergence and Practice of Treating Gender*. New York: New York University Press, 2021.

Young, Rebecca M., and Katrina Karkazis. *Testosterone: An Unauthorized Biography*. Cambridge, MA: Harvard University Press, 2022.

Black Trans and Trans People of Color

Bailey, Marlon M. *Butch Queens Up in Pumps: Gender, Performance, and Ballroom Culture in Detroit*. Ann Arbor: University of Michigan Press, 2013.

Bey, Marquis. *Black Trans Feminism*. Durham, NC: Duke University Press, 2022.

Cardenas, Micha. *Poetic Operations: Trans of Color Art in Digital Media*. Durham, NC: Duke University Press, 2022.

Chen, Jian Neo. *Trans Exploits: Trans of Color Cultures and Technologies in Movement*. Durham, NC: Duke University Press Books, 2019.

Choudrey, Sabah. *Supporting Trans People of Colour: How to Make Your Practice Inclusive*. Philadelphia: Jessica Kingsley Publishers, 2022.

Ellison, Treva, Kai M. Green, Matt Richardson, and C. Riley Snorton. "We Got Issues: Toward a Black Trans*/Studies." *TSQ: Transgender Studies Quarterly* 4, no. 2 (May 1, 2017): 162–69.

Galarte, Francisco J. *Brown Trans Figurations: Rethinking Race, Gender, and Sexuality in Chicanx/Latinx Studies*. Austin: University of Texas Press, 2021.

Glover, Julian Kevon. "Customer Service Representatives: Sex Work among Black Transgender Women in Chicago's Ballroom Scene." *South Atlantic Quarterly* 120, no. 3 (July 1, 2021): 553–71.

Hayward, Eva S. "Don't Exist." *TSQ: Transgender Studies Quarterly* 4, no. 2 (May 1, 2017): 191–94.

Snorton, C. Riley. *Black on Both Sides: A Racial History of Trans Identity*. 3rd ed. Minneapolis: University of Minnesota Press, 2017.

Tinsley, Omise'eke Natasha. *Ezili's Mirrors: Imagining Black Queer Genders*. Durham, NC: Duke University Press, 2018.

Trans and Nonbinary Children and Youth

Gill-Peterson, Jules. *Histories of the Transgender Child*. Minneapolis: University of Minnesota Press, 2018.

Meadow, Tey. *Trans Kids: Being Gendered in the Twenty-First Century*. Berkeley: University of California Press, 2017.

Rahilly, Elizabeth. *Trans-Affirmative Parenting: Raising Kids across the Gender Spectrum*. New York: New York University Press, 2020.

Travers. *The Trans Generation: How Trans Kids (and Their Parents) Are Creating a Gender Revolution*. New York: New York University Press, 2018.

Key Texts in Trans Studies

Adair, Cassius, Cameron Awkward-Rich, and Amy Marvin. "Before Trans Studies." *TSQ: Transgender Studies Quarterly* 7, no. 3 (August 1, 2020): 306–20.

Awkward-Rich, Cameron. "Trans, Feminism: *Or,* Reading like a Depressed Transsexual." *Signs: Journal of Women in Culture and Society* 42, no. 4 (June 1, 2017): 819–41.

Bettcher, Talia Mae. "Trapped in the Wrong Theory: Rethinking Trans Oppression and Resistance." *Signs: Journal of Women in Culture and Society* 39, no. 2 (January 1, 2014): 383–406.

Chu, Andrea Long, and Emmett Harsin Drager. "After Trans Studies." *TSQ: Transgender Studies Quarterly* 6, no. 1 (February 1, 2019): 103–16.

Gossett, Che, and Eva Hayward. "Trans in a Time of HIV/AIDS." *TSQ: Transgender Studies Quarterly* 7, no. 4 (November 1, 2020): 527–53.

Halberstam, Jack. *Female Masculinity.* 20th anniversary ed. Durham, NC: Duke University Press, 2019.

Namaste, Viviane. *Invisible Lives: The Erasure of Transsexual and Transgendered People.* Chicago: University of Chicago Press, 2000.

Preciado, Paul B. *Testo Junkie: Sex, Drugs, and Biopolitics in the Pharmacopornographic Era.* Translated by Bruce Benderson. New York: Feminist Press, 2013.

Prosser, Jay. *Second Skins: The Body Narratives of Transsexuality.* New York: Columbia University Press, 1998.

Stone, Sandy. "The Empire Strikes Back: A Posttranssexual Manifesto." *Camera Obscura: Feminism, Culture, and Media Studies* 10, no. 2 (May 1, 1992): 150–76.

Stryker, Susan. "Introduction: Trans* Studies Now." *TSQ: Transgender Studies Quarterly* 7, no. 3 (August 1, 2020): 299–305.

———. "My Words to Victor Frankenstein above the Village of Chamounix—Performing Transgender Rage." *GLQ: A Journal of Lesbian and Gay Studies* 1, no. 3 (June 1, 1994): 237–54.

———. "Transgender Studies: Queer Theory's Evil Twin." *GLQ: A Journal of Lesbian and Gay Studies* 10, no. 2 (2004): 212–15.

Global South, Non-Western, and Decolonial Perspectives

Aizura, Aren Z. *Mobile Subjects: Transnational Imaginaries of Gender Reassignment.* Durham, NC: Duke University Press Books, 2018.

Chiang, Howard. *Transtopia in the Sinophone Pacific.* New York: Columbia University Press, 2021.

Driskill, Qwo-Li. *Asegi Stories: Cherokee Queer and Two-Spirit Memory.* Tucson: University of Arizona Press, 2016.

Kauanui, J. Kehaulani. *Paradoxes of Hawaiian Sovereignty: Land, Sex, and the Colonial Politics of State Nationalism.* Durham, NC: Duke University Press, 2018.

La Fontaine–Stokes, Lawrence. *Trans Locas: The Politics of Puerto Rican Drag and Trans Performance.* Ann Arbor: University of Michigan Press, 2021.

Manalansan, Martin F., IV. *Global Divas: Filipino Gay Men in the Diaspora.* Durham, NC: Duke University Press, 2003.

Miranda, Deborah A. (Ohlone-Costanoan Esselen Nation, Chumash). "Extermination of the Joyas: Gendercide in Spanish California." *GLQ: A Journal of Lesbian and Gay Studies* 16, no. 1 (2010): 253–84.

Ramberg, Lucinda. *Given to the Goddess: South Indian Devadasis and the Sexuality of Religion.* Durham, NC: Duke University Press, 2014.

Reddy, Gayatri. *With Respect to Sex: Negotiating Hijra Identity in South India.* Chicago: University of Chicago Press, 2005.

Saria, Vaibhav. *Hijras, Lovers, Brothers: Surviving Sex and Poverty in Rural India.* New York: Fordham University Press, 2021.

Towle, Evan B., and Lynn Marie Morgan. "Romancing the Transgender Native: Rethinking the Use of the 'Third Gender' Concept." *GLQ: A Journal of Lesbian and Gay Studies* 8, no. 4 (2002): 469–97.

Williams, Walter L. L. *Spirit and the Flesh: Sexual Diversity in American Indian Culture.* Boston: Beacon Press, 1992.

ROBERTO L. ABREU (he/him/él) is an Assistant Professor of Counseling Psychology in the Department of Psychology at the University of Florida. His research explores ways in which marginalized communities resist systemic oppression and promote *bienestar colectivo* (collective well-being), with a particular focus on Latinx communities; lesbian, gay, bisexual, transgender, and queer (LGBTQ) people; and the intersection of Latinx and LGBTQ people and communities.

CATHERINE ARMSTRONG earned a BA and MA in History at the University of Warwick, where she stayed to do her PhD, supervised by Professor Bernard Capp, and wrote her thesis "Place and Potential in New World Travel Literature, 1607–1660." In 2014 Dr. Armstrong joined Loughborough University as a Lecturer and, since 2021, as a Reader in Modern History. Dr. Armstrong is a historian of colonial North America and the United States in the eighteenth and nineteenth centuries and of the history of slavery in a transnational context. In the field of book history, she is coeditor, with John Hinks, of the journal *Publishing History*. Dr. Armstrong is also working on a project to create an archive of oral histories of the trans community of the East Midlands of England.

SHEREE BEKKER (she/her), PhD, is an Assistant Professor in the Department for Health at the University of Bath and a member of the Centre for Health and Injury and Illness Prevention in Sport. Her transdisciplinary research contributes critical insights across a range of contemporary challenges in sport and exercise medicine, with a focus on those in sports injury prevention. Her current research is focused on two key strands: (1) understanding the influence of gendered environments on sports injury and (2) conceptualizing gender-inclusive sport. She takes a translational approach to this research, with the aim of providing considerations that are useful in policy and practice. Bekker received the 2019 *British Journal of Sports Medicine* Editor's Choice Academy Award for her PhD research.

STACY BRANHAM is an Assistant Professor of Informatics at the University of California, Irvine. Her research reveals how technology can isolate, offend, and harm people with disabilities, as much as it has the potential to integrate and empower them when properly designed. Her work has been recognized with several awards for best paper at top research conferences and has been supported by more than $15 million from funding entities, including the Jacobs Foundation, Toyota, Intel, and the National Science Foundation. In 2021 she received the NSF CAREER Award and was named one of the "Brilliant 10" rising STEM researchers by *Popular Science*.

CHRISTOPHER CARPENTER is a health and labor economist who studies the effects of public policies on health and family outcomes. He is President-Elect of the Association for Public Policy Analysis and Management, former Vice President of the Southern Economic Association, a former member of the Board of Directors of the American Society of Health Economists, and Cofounder and Co-chair of the American Economic Association's Committee on the Status of LGBTQ+ Individuals in the Economics Profession. At Vanderbilt University he directs the Program in Public Policy Studies and the TIPS (Trans-Institutional Programs)–supported Vanderbilt LGBTQ+ Policy Lab, and he is the faculty facilitator for Q&A (Queer & Asian).

L. F. CARVER is a multidisciplinary health researcher with a PhD in Sociology and an MA in Psychology. The overarching question that guides Dr. Carver's research is "What are the factors that impact health and well-being, especially in older age?" Using an intersectional lens and situated within the One Health perspective, Dr. Carver's research and writing considers impacts of the human-animal bond as it intersects with gender, age, and social determinants of health, as well as issues surrounding technology, privacy, and surveillance. Dr. Carver is also interested in the reciprocal interaction between humans and farmed, wild, abandoned, and/or feral nonhuman animal populations and the well-being of those populations.

MANDY COLES focuses on adolescent issues, care for gender-non-conforming youth, reproductive health, and contraception. Coles's research interests include pregnancy prevention, gender-nonconforming youth, intrauterine devices and contraceptive implants (LARC), and pregnancy assessment. She completed a residency at Baystate Medical Center Children's Hospital in Springfield, Massachusetts, in 2006, followed in 2009 by a Fellowship in Adolescent Medicine at the University of Rochester School of Medicine & Dentistry in Rochester, New York.

ARIN COLLIN, MD, is a Medical Resident at the University of California, Riverside, School of Medicine. Her academic interests are outcomes of gender-affirming care, treatment of borderline personality disorder, and clinical talk therapy. Her undergraduate study spanned biology, philosophy, and psychology. She previously served as a Petty Officer in the US Navy and has volunteered with numerous organizations providing food, housing, and health care to the economically disadvantaged. Her hobbies include wrenching on her motorcycle and playing *Mario Kart* with her wife.

GEORGE B. CUNNINGHAM is a Professor and Chair of the Department of Sport Management at the University of Florida. He is also Director of the Laboratory for Diversity in Sport. Author of over 200 articles and book chapters, Cunningham conducts research in the area of diversity and inclusion in sport and physical activity. He is a past president of the North American Society for Sport Management and a fellow of the National Academy of Kinesiology.

AVERY DAME-GRIFF is a Lecturer in Women's and Gender Studies at Gonzaga University, as well as the primary curator of the Queer Digital History Project (queerdigital.com), an independent community history project preserving information on early LGBTQ communities. His book *The Two Revolutions* (forthcoming from New York University Press) tracks how the internet transformed transgender political organizing from the 1980s to the contemporary moment. His work has appeared in *Internet Histories, Feminist Media Studies,* the *Journal of Language and Sexuality, Critical Studies in Media Communication,* and *TSQ: Transgender Studies Quarterly.*

JULES GILL-PETERSON is a scholar of transgender history and the history of sexuality, focusing on racial histories of sex, gender, and trans embodiment spanning both institutional and vernacular science and medicine. Gill-Peterson is the author of *Histories of the Transgender Child* (University of Minnesota Press, 2018) and recipient of a Lambda Literary Award for Transgender Nonfiction and the Children's Literature Association Book Award. The book was the first to challenge the myth that transgender children are a new phenomenon in the twenty-first century. She is an Associate Professor of History at Johns Hopkins University.

ABBIE E. GOLDBERG is a Professor of Clinical Psychology at Clark University. A central theme of her research is the decentering of any "normal" or "typical" family, sexuality, or gender, to allow room for diverse families, sexualities, and genders. For 15 years, Dr. Goldberg has been conducting a longitudinal study of adoptive families headed by female, male, and heterosexual couples, which focuses in part on families' experiences in the school setting. She also conducts research on the higher education experiences of trans and gender-nonconforming individuals, postpartum well-being in women with diverse sexual histories, and relationship dissolution and divorce in diverse families.

GILBERT GONZALES, PhD, MHA, is an Assistant Professor in the Department of Medicine, Health & Society, the Program for Public Policy Studies, and the Department of Health Policy at Vanderbilt University. Professor Gonzales's research examines how public policies affect health outcomes, access to care, and health disparities for lesbian, gay, bisexual, transgender, queer, and questioning populations. He also studies the impact of health care reforms on vulnerable populations. His research has appeared in the *American Journal of Public Health*, *Pediatrics*, *JAMA*, *Health Affairs*, the *Milbank Quarterly*, and the *New England Journal of Medicine*.

FRANCES GRIMSTAD (she/her), Assistant Professor of Gynecology at Boston Children's Hospital and Harvard Medical School, engages in clinical and research work surrounding transgender and intersex reproductive health. She has been involved in trans health advocacy since her own adolescence, when she decided to pursue medicine to address disparities in care faced by these communities. Her interests center around optimizing reproductive health outcomes for both populations with regard to hormonal and menstrual management, surgical care, and family planning.

FOAD HAMIDI is an Assistant Professor in Information Systems at the University of Maryland, Baltimore County. He directs the Designing pARticipatory futurEs (DARE) Lab. He researches human-computer interaction with a focus on participatory design and evaluation of emerging interactive systems. He also pursues research in using DIY (do-it-yourself) and maker approaches to facilitate creativity, learning, and empowerment for children and youth with and without disabilities. He has a PhD in Computer Science from the Lassonde School of Engineering at York University in Toronto, Canada.

ELIZABETH HEINEMAN is a Professor of History and of Gender, Women's, and Sexuality Studies at the University of Iowa. She received her PhD from the University of North Carolina at Chapel Hill in 1993 and was the 2010 recipient of the AICGS/DAAD Prize for Distinguished Scholarship in German and European Studies. Her books include *What Difference Does a Husband Make? Women and Marital Status in Nazi and Postwar Germany, Before Porn Was Legal: The Erotica Empire of Beate Uhse, The History of Sexual Violence in Conflict Zones: From the Ancient World to the Era of Human Rights*, and the memoir *Ghostbelly*.

GLEN HOSKING is an Associate Professor of Psychology at La Trobe University. He is a clinical psychologist, researcher, and educator. Hosking completed his Doctorate in Psychology at the Australian Catholic University in 2003. His work since then has been in a range of positions in academic and treatment environments as a clinical psychologist and lecturer in psychology.

BETHANY GRACE HOWE has a PhD and is an independent researcher working with the NLGJA: The Association of LGBTQ Journalists, where she is also a board member. In this capacity she's worked with numerous media outlets to help inform their transgender coverage, including CNN, Politico, and Vox. As a researcher, media specialist, and transgender woman, she works to understand the effect of media-based and interpersonally communicated microaggressions on transgender people. When she's not researching, she enjoys spending time with her daughter, Nola, whom she calls her "Mini-Me."

JAY A. IRWIN has a PhD in Medical Sociology, and his research examines LGBTQ+ health, specifically the health of lesbians and transgender people. Irwin's dissertation focused on the experience of stress and discrimination among lesbians in the southeastern United States. His most recent work includes a statewide survey on the health of LGBTQ+ people living in Nebraska, the experience of being trans and living in Nebraska in relation to localized gender norms, and leadership development for LGBTQ+ young professionals.

SHANNA K. KATTARI, PhD, MEd, CSE, ACS, is an Associate Professor at the University of Michigan's School of Social Work and the Department of Women and Gender Studies and is the Director of the [Sexuality|Relationships|Gender] Research Collective. A White, Jewish, nonbinary, disabled, chronically ill, neurodivergent, middle-class queer fat Femme, their practice and community background is as a board-certified sexologist, certified sexuality educator, and social justice advocate. Dr. Kattari's research focuses on understanding how power, privilege, and oppression systematically marginalize, exclude, and discriminate against people regarding their identities/expressions through negative attitudes, policies reinforcing oppression, oppressive actions, and isolation.

KACIE KIDD is a board-certified Pediatrician, Internist, and a specialist in adolescent medicine as well as an Assistant Professor of Pediatrics and Internal Medicine at the West Virginia University School of Medicine. She serves as the Medical Director of the WVU Medicine Children's Gender & Sexual Development Clinic. Dr. Kidd is also a researcher focused on mixed-methods studies to better understand the experiences of gender-diverse and other marginalized youth and their families in order to develop interventions that improve health equity. Her research has been published in prestigious peer-reviewed journals, and she has been an invited speaker at regional, national, and international conferences.

TERRY S. KOGAN is a Professor of Law Emeritus at the University of Utah's S.J. Quinney College of Law. He has taught in the areas of civil procedure, contracts, intellectual property, trusts and estates, art law, legal philosophy, and sexuality and the law. He has spent the past two decades considering the rights of transgender people, in particular issues surrounding the legal and cultural norms that mandate the segregation of public restrooms by sex. In addition, he has explored issues related to photography and copyright law.

VANESSA LOBUE, PhD, is a Professor of Psychology at Rutgers University. She received her BS from Carnegie Mellon University and her MA and PhD from the University of Virginia. Dr. LoBue's research focuses on human behavioral responses to emotionally valenced stimuli—specifically to negative or threatening stimuli—and the mechanisms guiding the development of these responses. In particular, she examines how early perceptual biases for threat contribute to maladaptive avoidance behaviors, such as those associated with the development of fear and anxiety, and how cognition contributes to children's learning of adaptive avoidance responses, such as avoiding contagious people or contaminated objects.

GABRIEL M. LOCKETT (he/him/his) is a doctoral student in counseling psychology in the University of Florida's Department of Psychology and a member of the Collective Healing and Empowering VoicEs through Research and Engagement (¡Chévere!) Lab. His research interests are centered on the psychological wellness of QT Black, Indigenous, People of Color.

MEGAN K. MAAS, PhD, is an Assistant Professor in Human Development & Family Studies at Michigan State University. Her award-winning research, recognized by the American Psychological Association and funded by the National Institutes of Health, focuses on media's impacts on adolescents' sexual and mental health. As a former health educator (turned academic), she has been training teachers, social workers, and school counselors on pornography use among teens for the last 10 years. In addition to publishing in academic journals, she also publishes her work in mass media outlets such as HuffPost, CNN, and Salon.

JULIE MANNING MAGID is a Professor of Business Law at Indiana University's Kelley School of Business in Indianapolis. Magid is also the Executive Associate Dean for the Kelley School and the Executive and Academic Director of the Randall L. Tobias Center for Leadership Excellence at Indiana University. Her areas of expertise include leadership, workplace dynamics (including innovation, diversity, and inclusion), governance, privacy, and ethics. Magid served as editor-in-chief of the *American Business Law Journal*. In addition, she is a Kelley Venture Fellow and the Life Sciences Research Fellow with the Center for the Business of Life Sciences. Magid attained degrees from the University of Michigan Law School and Georgetown University.

EM MATSUNO (they/them), PhD, is an Assistant Professor in Counseling and Counseling Psychology at Arizona State University. Dr. Matsuno's primary research goals are twofold: (1) to understand the minority stressors and resilience factors that Two-spirit, trans, and nonbinary (2STNB) people experience and (2) to develop and test interventions to reduce minority stressors and/or increase resilience factors for 2STNB people. Specific interests include family acceptance and parental support of 2STNB youth, nonbinary people, 2STNB graduate students and career seekers, and 2STNB people of color.

TEY MEADOW is an Associate Professor of Sociology at Columbia University. Her work focuses on a broad range of issues, including the emergence of the transgender child as a social category, the international politics of family diversity, the creation and maintenance of legal gender classifications, and the ways that individuals negotiate sex and power in intimate relationships. Meadow is the author of *Trans Kids: Being Gendered in the Twenty-First Century* (University of California Press, 2018) and the coeditor of *Other, Please Specify: Queer Methods in Sociology* (University of California Press, 2018).

KYL MYERS is a PhD-trained sociologist, award-winning educator, and globally recognized advocate for gender creative parenting. Dr. Myers creates online gender-education resources that are free to the public and is the author of *Raising Them: Our Adventure in Gender Creative Parenting*. Myers is an Adjunct Assistant Professor in the Sociology Department at the University of Utah and works with global organizations that want to build a more inclusive and equitable world. Myers is genderqueer, uses they/them and she/her pronouns, and lives and plays with their family, moving between the United States and Australia.

MADELEINE PAPE is a sociologist and Olympian who competed for Australia in the 800 meters event at the 2008 Summer Olympics in Beijing. Pape completed her PhD in Sociology at the University of Wisconsin–Madison in 2019 and is currently a Postdoctoral Researcher at the Institute of Sport Sciences at the University of Lausanne. She has published in some of the leading journals of her field, including *Gender & Society, Social Studies of Science, Body & Society,* and the *Sociology of Sport Journal.*

RUTH PEARCE is a Lecturer in Community Development at the University of Glasgow. Her research explores themes of inequality, marginalization, power, and transformative political struggle from a trans feminist perspective. She is the author of *Understanding Trans Health* (Policy Press, 2018) and coeditor of *The Emergence of Trans* (Routledge, 2019) and *TERF Wars* (Sage, 2020). Ruth blogs and shares free copies of her work on her website at http://ruthpearce.net.

JAE A. PUCKETT, PhD, is an Assistant Professor in the Department of Psychology at Michigan State University. Their research documents experiences of stigma and marginalization encountered by transgender and gender-diverse individuals and the negative health outcomes of prejudice using qualitative, quantitative, and mixed-methods approaches. Their research provides a nuanced understanding of the mechanisms and processes that underlie the production of health disparities in this community, as well as strategies for coping and being resilient in the face of stigma.

G. SAMANTHA ROSENTHAL (she/they) is an Associate Professor of History and the Coordinator of the Public History Concentration at Roanoke College in Salem, Virginia. She is the author of two books, *Living Queer History: Remembrance and Belonging in a Southern City* and *Beyond Hawai'i: Native Labor in the Pacific World.* They are cofounder of the Southwest Virginia LGBTQ+ History Project, a nationally recognized queer public history initiative. Her work has received awards and recognition from the National Council on Public History, the Oral History Association, the Committee on LGBT History, the American Society for Environmental History, and the Working-Class Studies Association.

MORGAN KLAUS SCHEUERMAN is a PhD student of information science at the University of Colorado Boulder and a 2021 Microsoft Research Fellow. His research focuses on the intersection of technical infrastructure and marginalized identities. In particular, he examines how gender and race characteristics are embedded in algorithmic infrastructures and how those permeations influence the entire system. His recent work explores how gender and race classification in computer vision technologies excludes and endangers at-risk individuals.

ELIZABETH A. SHARROW, PhD, MPP, is an Associate Professor of Public Policy and History at the University of Massachusetts Amherst's School of Public Policy. Her research explores the politics of Title IX and the ways that public policy shapes understandings of sex and gender at the intersections of race, sexuality, ability, and class. She is currently working on a book manuscript, provisionally titled "Allowed to Play but Not to Win," which explores the history of sex-segregated athletics under Title IX. She has published research on the politics of sex, gender, and fatherhood and the politics of college sport in the United States. Her research has been funded by the National Science Foundation, the Social Science Research Council, and the American Association of University Women, among other sources.

CARL SHEPERIS, PhD, serves as the Dean of the College of Education and Human Development at Texas A&M University–San Antonio. Dr. Sheperis has extensive experience in pediatric and family mental health and has published over 100 papers and 8 books. In 2018 Dr. Sheperis was named a fellow of the American Counseling Association.

DONNA SHEPERIS, PhD, is a Professor at Palo Alto University. She earned her PhD in Counselor Education from the University of Mississippi and her Masters in Counseling from Delta State University. She is a Licensed Professional Counselor in Arizona and Texas, a board-certified Counselor, a board-certified Clinical Mental Health Counselor, a board-certified TeleMental Health Provider, and an Approved Clinical Supervisor with 30 years of experience in clinical mental health counseling settings. She specializes in working with adult mental health needs.

stef m. shuster is an Assistant Professor in Lyman Briggs College and the Department of Sociology at Michigan State University. Their current research in gender, medicine, and feminist science and technology studies considers how evidence and expertise are constructed, mobilized, and weaponized, which is the subject of their book *Trans Medicine: The Emergence and Practice of Treating Gender* (New York University Press, 2021). In *Trans Medicine*, shuster traces the development of this medical field from the 1950s to contemporary times to show how providers create and use scientific and medical evidence and expertise to "treat" a gender identity and uphold their authority.

JULES SOSTRE (them/them/theirs and she/her/hers) is a doctoral student in counseling psychology in the University of Florida's Department of Psychology and a member of the Collective Healing and Empowering VoicEs through Research and Engagement (¡Chévere!) Lab. They are devoted to continuing to work and advocate for Queer and/or Trans Communities of Color throughout their life.

RYAN STORR, PhD, is a Research Fellow with the Sport Innovation Research group at Swinburne University. Previously, he was a Lecturer and Academic Course Advisor in Sport Development at Western Sydney University. He completed his PhD at Victoria University, where his thesis explored how community sports clubs respond to diversity and engage in diversity work. He has led several recent research projects, specifically around LGBTI+ inclusion in sport, with the most recent being a funded evaluation exploring the current level of LGBTI+ inclusion within an Australian sporting code. Ryan is also the cofounder of the LGBTI+ sport charity Proud 2 Play.

CARL STREED JR., MD, MPH, is an Assistant Professor in the Boston University School of Medicine. After attending medical school and serving a residency in internal medicine at Johns Hopkins University, he completed a fellowship in general internal medicine at Brigham and Women's Hospital. Nationally, he has chaired the American Medical Association Advisory Committee on LGBTQ Issues and served on the board of GLMA: Health Professionals Advancing LGBTQ Equality. As Research Lead for the Center for Transgender Medicine and Surgery at Boston Medical Center, he collaborates with researchers, clinicians, and community to assess and address the health and well-being of transgender and gender-diverse individuals.

DIANA M. TORDOFF, PhD, MPH, is a Postdoctoral Scholar with The PRIDE Study at Stanford University's School of Medicine. Dr. Tordoff earned a PhD and MPH in Epidemiology at the University of Washington and has over ten years' experience working with LGBTQ communities. Her research interests include LGBTQ+ health equity, sexual health and HIV/STI prevention, and community-based participatory research methods.

TRAVERS is a Professor of Sociology at Simon Fraser University. Their recent book, *The Trans Generation: How Trans Kids (and Their Parents) Are Creating a Gender Revolution*, situates trans kids in Canada and the United States, white settler nations characterized by significant social inequality. In addition to a central research focus on transgender children and youth, Dr. Travers has published extensively on the relationship between sport and social justice, with particular emphasis on the inclusion and exclusion of women and queer and trans people of all ages. Dr. Travers is Deputy Editor of the journal *Gender & Society*.

Index

affirming care, 142–43, 158, 161, 162; pay gaps for trans people, 119, 207

gatekeeping, in trans health care, xvii, 18–19, 77, 103, 140–43

Gay Liberation Front, 194

gay rights: and assumption of trans rights progress, 4; in Germany, 22, 24–25; and marriage, 199; and Stonewall riots, xx, 194; and trans liberation movement, 194–96

gender: defined, 48, 90; development of term, 8, 146; and health outcomes, 145–48; in identity development, 89–93; recognition by artificial intelligence, 215–20; resistant to environmental intervention, 102; segregated restrooms, 44, 52–57; vs. sex, 6, 8, 47–48, 90–91, 145–46, 182; vs. sexual orientation, 147; as social construct, 48, 90, 146; understanding of concept, 5–6

gender-affirming care: defined, xvii, 151; disinformation on, 97–98; first surgeries in, 138; and gatekeeping, xvii, 18–19, 77, 103, 140–43; generational differences in seeking, 66, 67; inequities in access to, xvii, 112–13, 136, 137–38, 142–43, 157–63; and insurance, 136–37, 142–43, 206; and mental health, 68–69, 129–32, 154, 158, 165, 184; and regrets, 97, 141; rise of model, 142, 158–59; safety of, 130–31; standards of care, 137–38; and waiting to transition, xvii–xviii, 84–85, 140–41. See also bans on gender-affirming care; hormone therapy; puberty blockers; surgery; treatment, traditional

gender-affirming care for youths: bans on, xv–xvi, 77, 132; barriers to, 131; inequities of access to, 157–63; and mental health, 129–32; and physicians, 150–56, 164–69

gender assignment at birth, 8, 42–44, 45, 117, 177–79

gender binary, policing of, 42–45, 192

gender clinics, 140–41

gender dysphoria: defined, 77, 98, 151; and gatekeeping, 77, 142–43; mental health risks of, 98, 114; and puberty, 151; "rapid onset," 97; surgery and reduction in, 154

gender expression, 11–14, 91–92

gender fluid, as term, 146

Genderline forum, 30

gender nonaffirmation. See misgendering

generational differences in gender identity, 32–33, 65–69, 98, 117, 182

Gentili, Ceclia, xxii

Gentleman Jack (Anne Lister), 13

Georgia, laws in, 173, 227

Gorsuch, Neil, 192, 201–3

harassment, in workplace, 202

Hawaiian trans history, 7, 14

Health and Human Services Office for Civil Rights, 225

health care system: discrimination in, 77, 136–37, 169, 181–85, 193, 225; evaluating colleges for, 124–25; and health care tourism, 137–38; insurance and insurers, 136–37, 142–43, 206; and staff training, 166–67, 168, 184–85; and trans people of color, 76–78, 182, 183–84; and trans rights, 195

heterosexuality and gatekeeping, 103, 140, 141

hijras, 6

Hirschfeld, Magnus, 21–26, 138

history, trans people in: Appalachia, 34–39; and colonialism, 6–7, 75–76; and early internet, 28–33; gender diversity of, 5–9; and medical treatment, 17–19; tipping point narrative, 4, 5; and visibility, 11–14; and youths, 16–20, 37, 39

Hopkins, Ann, 202

hormone levels and sex identity, 177–79

hormone therapy: defined, 130; development of, 138; and mental health, 131; and nonbinary people, 154; physician training on, 166–67, 168; safety of, 154; and youths, 153, 154, 162

House of G, xx, xxiii

housework, gendered, 118–19

housing: gender-inclusive, on college campuses, 124; and trans discrimination, 43, 182, 224

Hubbard, Laurel, 232–33